If you've ever felt like you were too busy to have fun, this book is for you. If, like me, you measure your worth by productivity and deep down you're unsure if you deserve fun, then this book is *definitely* for you. I got teary in the first chapter. Mandy's words will speak to your heart, and if you are open to thinking differently, they could change your life.

LISA LEONARD, jewelry designer and author

As a recovering perfectionist, I'm often so worried about failing that I forget to enjoy this one beautiful life God gave me. Mandy's book is a poignant, insightful, hilarious reminder to make room for joyful absurdity. My mind is already swimming with ideas of how to have more fun with my kids, my marriage, and my job!

JJ HELLER, singer and songwriter

I'll admit, I consider myself a fun person. I am always looking for the next fun thing to do. My Instagram profile reads, "pretty good at laughing," and I never take myself too seriously. But as the saying goes, "life happens," and days fill up, and the to-do list is far too long, and I can forget about the fun. Mandy's book *Have More Fun* is a sweet reminder for me about how much I love having fun and how easily fun can fit into every corner of my daily life, even when I may feel too busy. Full of silly stories and easy ways to incorporate fun into our day-to-day, this book is an important reminder for all of us.

HEATHER AVIS, author, influencer,
shouter of worth

In a world that pushes us to run harder/faster/stronger, *Have More Fun* offers us a daring, amped-up drumbeat to dance to along the way. For the overworked and underwhelmed, join Mandy Arioto as she turns up the volume to hear the jubilant lyrics many of us have long forgotten.

ERIN LOECHNER, author of *Chasing Slow*
and founder of OtherGoose.com

Mandy writes, "I don't want to get to the end of my life and realize that the best thing about me was that I was really good at keeping up with my email." Yikes. She totally got me. Right. Where. I. Live. I'm great at emails and less great at fun. Okay, I'm not terrible at having fun. But here in Mandy's honest, inviting, winsome, and playful style I see what I haven't before. Beyond playing with grandkids. Beyond entertaining audiences. Beyond my hobby of reading or walking my dogs. A divine version of life-giving fun is waiting for me in the here and now of my everyday. And I'm going to embrace it.

ELISA MORGAN, speaker, author, *The Prayer Coin, The
Beauty of Broken,* President Emerita, MOPS International

Ever gotten to the end of a week, or month, or OH MY GOOD-NESS . . . YEAR, and realized that while you've accomplished plenty you've forgotten to enjoy the journey? Been there! I have good news though. Mandy Arioto has penned a resource that is inspiring, encouraging, hilarious, and chock full of fabulous ideas for adding fun and meaning to nine areas of your current life. She'll have you laughing one minute and crying the next, in the best way. I read every word, and this book is worth your time.

SANDRA STANLEY, author and speaker

HAVE MORE FUN

HAVE MORE
FUN

HOW TO BE REMARKABLE,
STOP FEELING STUCK, AND
START ENJOYING LIFE

MANDY ARIOTO

ZONDERVAN

Have More Fun
Copyright © 2019 by MOPS International, Inc.

Requests for information should be addressed to:
Zondervan, *3900 Sparks Dr. SE, Grand Rapids, Michigan 49546*

ISBN 978-0-310-34043-0 (softcover)

ISBN 978-0-310-35537-3 (audio)

ISBN 978-0-310-34045-4 (ebook)

Cover photography: Erica Krysl
Interior design: Kait Lamphere

Printed in the United States of America

18 19 20 21 22 23 24 /LSC/ 15 14 13 12 11 10 9 8 7 6 5 4 3 2 1

To Joseph, Elle, and Charlotte,
who are my favorite part of any day.

CONTENTS

FOREWORD

A few years ago my professional bio simply read: "attorney," "diplomat," and "nonprofit founder."

Reading it sort of made me want to take a nap.

So when I'd meet new acquaintances, and I'd crack a joke or notice something completely absurd, they'd often glance past me in search of the real grown-up. That's why, for the sake of transparency, I changed the bio to say: "Chief of Fun & Whimsy."

It felt more honest.

If you were to ask the people who know me best in this world what my *one thing* is—what wakes me up every morning, propels me through the day, and rattles around in my head at night before I fall asleep—most of them would say *love*. It's my thing. It really is.

It's what I was made for, and it's what you were made for.

But if you'd only known me a few minutes, if you were that handshaker—shaking your head and wondering what sort of shenanigans would unfold should I be allowed to speak in a court of law—you might also make the reasonable guess that my thing, my *one* thing, was *fun*.

And you wouldn't be entirely wrong.

I don't really like to draw hard and fast lines between love and fun. In my life, and in my family's life, the two are often tangled up together.

Before my wife Maria and I got married, we discussed what our future might look like. Specifically, we began to imagine *how* we would live. And we decided together that we wanted joy and whimsy and fun to be central to the life we shared and to the family we were building. So when our daughter Lindsey was ten, and we saw $99 airline tickets to London, we decided I should take her to London for a tea party. As one does.

Another weekend I purchased a radio-controlled airplane and dragged the kids outside for our plane's maiden voyage. As you might imagine, it was totally *awesome*! It was awesome for all forty-five seconds before I flew that plane into a tree (which, of course, was actually also kind of cool). I wasn't worried about Maria's reaction to wasting the money, because . . . well . . . *fun*. It's one of the things we'd chosen to be about.

You can choose fun too.

You can choose it for yourself, and if you've got a family of folks who are willing to play along, you can choose it with them.

Deciding to embrace fun is what Mandy Arioto has done, and it's what she can help you do.

One of many things I love about Mandy is that she has chosen to be about what matters most (and by that, of course, I mean fun. Obviously. And love). She's been intentional about both of those priorities because there was a moment in her life when she recognized a joy deficit. She noticed that she was only allowing herself to have fun after the things on her to-do list were complete. That she'd been prioritizing productivity over delight. And, in that moment, pausing to look forward and imagine the rest of her days on this earth, she considered whether she needed a new trajectory.

Do I want to check a lot of tasks off of lists, or do I want to celebrate the wonderful life I've been given and invite others to embrace joy along the way?

So Mandy did something similar to what sweet Maria and I had done years earlier: she committed to living the rest of her days prioritizing fun, love, and legacy.

Mandy has written *Have More Fun* for you because she is convinced that fun matters. And she's persuaded that, in ways that can't quite be quantified, tiny moments reshape people's hearts. Including yours.

If you're game, fun can change your life.

It can change the lives of the people you love.

And it can change the lives of people you've not yet met, but who you were made to love.

Does that opportunity make you as amped as it makes me?

Mandy is inviting you to kick off your shoes, ignore

whatever your law-abiding neighbors might think about you, and join her on this journey.

Say yes.

Your neighbors need you to say yes. Your family needs you to say yes. The world needs you to say yes.

And know that as you choose to live with joy and delight and whimsy and fun, I'm cheering you on.

Bob Goff

INTRODUCTION

I grew up in a home where, every Saturday morning after eating breakfast together, my parents would look across the table with a glint of mischief in their eyes and tell my brother and me to "go outside and have an adventure, and don't come back until you do."

This means that I did a lot of really dumb stuff.

It also means that I used to be really good at having fun. That is, until I became an adult. No one prepped me for the fact that 82 percent of adulting is admin, and the other 18 percent is making food for other people and asking your kids, "How did this get wet?"

Very unintentionally, between making babies, building a career, and figuring out how things got wet, my priorities became checking things off my to-do list and getting stuff done.

I have spent most of my adult life waiting to have fun. I'll focus on fun once my work is caught up or when I feel rested, but up to this point neither of those things has happened. I can't tell you how many times I have missed playing with my kids to put one more load of laundry in. *If I had more time, I'd have more fun*, I told myself, but it wasn't the truth. I was lying straight to my face, because the alternative felt too big to admit.

I had simply forgotten to have fun.

I realized I had a problem when a coworker came in to my office one morning and said, "I just wanted to check on you because you were kind of a hot mess yesterday." To which I responded, "First of all, thanks for calling me hot."

But the truth is, I *was* a mess the day before, and a lot of days before that.

The previous month I had been on twelve different airplanes, staying up until two o'clock in the morning almost every night, sorting out work emergencies. On top of that, my kids had started teasing me because they said my laugh sounded fake, like I was going through the motions and pretending I was amused but that I had lost my playfulness. They were lighthearted in their approach, but I knew there was truth behind their joking.

Sometimes it takes a coworker calling you a hot mess to realize that you have completely forgotten to enjoy your life. I decided that day that I don't want to get to the end of my life and look back and realize that the best thing about me was that I was really good at keeping up with email. I want to have more fun now; I want to live with passion and stop taking life so seriously. I want to do crazy awesome things to show people I love them. I want my husband to look forward to falling into bed with me at the end of a long day. I want to make my kids laugh, and I want to start truly experiencing what it means to be loved by a good God, because that changes everything.

This was the catalyst for making one of the most important decisions I have ever made, right behind choosing a spouse and getting my eyebrows micro-bladed (kidding, but still life changing). I declared that my only goal for the next year was to have more fun. Now, I know it sounds too simple, but let me tell you it has changed everything, from how I parent to how I interact with people who annoy me.

What I have learned over the past year is that fun is the solution to so many of the things we worry about the most:

How do I get more done?

How do I parent in meaningful ways?

How do I make friends?

How can I find my purpose?

How do I spice up my sex life?

How do I adapt when things don't go as planned?

How do I improve my marriage?

Get unstuck?

The answer to every single one of these questions is as predictable as *c.* on a multiple-choice test: it's *fun,* and scientists agree.

Stanford University happiness expert Emma Seppälä says, "If we focus on boosting fun and happiness in our lives, even in little ways, research suggests we can end up more productive, charismatic, energetic, and innovative."[1] Let me break this down. All the research presented throughout this book suggests that if we have more fun we will accomplish more, be healthier, like ourselves better, and people will want to be our friend. Not to mention that fun is an aphrodisiac, the solution for online bullying, and the answer to almost every existential question about how to live a more fulfilling life.

If you have forgotten that fun is an option, or if you are feeling numb, bored, or simply ready for a change, fun is the answer, and the more of it the better. It is all around you, all the time, and you don't have to get all that other stuff done before you pay attention to it.

The average human being lives 30,000 days.[2] As of today, I have already lived 14,622 of those days, been married for 6,791, and been a parent for 6,119 of them. Giving a number to each of your days has a way of reprioritizing what you want to focus on. I used to think that I could anticipate what my days would bring, but life has taken so many disorienting and unexpected turns. My present life would have been unimaginable by my past self. So instead of overthinking them, overplanning them, or pretending I can control them, I am focused on having more fun with the days I am given. I have taken them far too seriously up until now. I hope I will have 20,075 more days to go, but I will remember that those days can worry about themselves. The only thing I need to do is make today extraordinary and a little more fun. We all have to go to the grocery store, so why not choose to have fun doing it?

In a time when politics, anxiety, mass shootings, racial tension, war, and suffering loop through our newsfeed, I am here to suggest that having more fun may be the solution. Together, we will look at science, theology, pop culture, and historical trends to dissect fun and suck as much magic from it as possible. This is your year to remember how much fun life can be.

Hold on tight, it's going to be a wild ride.

CHAPTER 1

WHEN YOU FORGET TO HAVE FUN

Are you breathing just a little and calling it a life?

MARY OLIVER

Here is a list of things I have forgotten recently:

On Pajama Day, I sent my kids to school in pajamas, only to find out when they got off the bus that afternoon that Pajama Day was the next day. Sorry, kids.

I cannot remember our Hulu password, so I keep resetting it and forgetting it again.

Speaking of Hulu, I recently declared a *Shark Tank*-worthy idea: "There should be a Hulu for books!" To which my husband replied, "You mean the library?" Oh yeah, forgot about that too.

Despite all the things I have forgotten over the years, there is one story from my childhood that I will never forget.

I grew up on a horse farm in upstate New York, which

is incredibly ironic because my mom was terrified of horses. It was my dad's lifelong dream, so my mom, being the good sport that she is, went along with it. My dad was always looking for new horses to add to our barn.

One day, Dad gets a call from a friend who knows a farmer in Pennsylvania who is wanting to sell two show horses. My dad gives the farmer a call, and after learning they are mares who come from a good line, decides it is worth a road trip to go and check them out.

The next weekend, my dad and I get up early and drive for four hours until we reach the driveway to the farm where the farmer is expecting us. My dad makes a right turn onto the long, winding street. On the right-hand side are meticulously maintained pastures stretching out for a half mile, filled with cows, goats, lush grass, and white fencing. I roll down my window to get a better view, and the sweet smell of freshly cut clover fills our car. We drive a little farther and come to an old white farmhouse flanked on the backside by a big red barn.

My dad parks the car in front of the house, and as we get out of the car, the farmer opens the front door of the house, making his way out to greet us. As he approaches my dad, we both glance at each other with mutual acknowledgment that we are surprised by how old he is, evidenced by his pace and the deep lines on his face.

Greeting us both with a hug, his deep voice booms, "Let me show you the girls."

Leading us back to the barn, he slides open the huge

door, and the scent of leather mixed with sawdust fills the air. I breathe deeply, because it is exactly how a barn should smell. Everything about the place is meticulous, just like the fields. We walk over to the horse stalls, and my dad pets the horses' manes, while the farmer fills him in on their personalities. My dad asks to see the horses run, so the old farmer opens their stalls and grabs both horses by their halters, leading them out the gate toward the pasture. One of the horses is so anxious to get out into the field that she shoves her nose between the gate and the fence post and flings it open, almost knocking me down. The two horses then proceed to run through the gate into the pasture, where they start bucking and chasing each other. They run to the farthest end of the field, roll in the dirt, and race back to a patch of lush grass. *Delight* is the only word that captures those horses in the pasture.

The minute my dad sees this, he looks straight at the farmer and says, "Yup, those are our girls."

At that point, I climb up on the top rung of the fence to get a better view of the horses, while my dad and the farmer talk terms. Our barn was in the process of being remodeled, so Dad tells the farmer that it would likely take another six weeks before we would be ready to bring the horses home.

The farmer waves a leathery hand worn rough from years of sowing hay and caring for animals in front of his face, and with a nod of his head says, "No problem at all. We'll take care of them until you're ready."

As building projects often do, our barn took longer to finish than my dad had estimated, and it wasn't until three months later that we retraced our route. But as we turned into the driveway of the farm, it looked different.

My dad looks at me out of the corner of his eye and asks, "Did I make a wrong turn?"

There are no animals in any of the pastures, the grass is so overgrown it is as tall as my waist, and everything looks to be in disrepair.

The farmer's wife greeted us as we got out of the car and then proceeded to tell us that a few days after our first trip, the farmer had gotten injured and hadn't been able to get out of bed. Because he couldn't farm, he didn't have the money to care for the animals. He was feeding them the bare minimum to keep them alive until he was back on his feet.

Realizing that the horses have been in their stalls for three months, my dad panics. He runs to the barn, flings open the door, and the stench of manure and urine is so strong I get sick to my stomach. He rushes over to the horses' stalls and realizes that the doors are the type that push in, but three months' worth of manure was blocking the doors from opening. I find some shovels, and for the next twenty minutes my dad and I shovel manure into a wheelbarrow.

Once we finally clear a way to free their doors, my dad looks at me and says, "Hey, remember how last time you almost got knocked over when they ran into the field? How about you climb up on those bales of hay so you are safe before I open their doors." I comply. Then, pushing the two doors open, my dad takes a step to the side so the two horses can run past him and into the open field.

The horses just stand there.

We grab lead lines and try to pull them out of their stalls.

They won't budge.

At this point my dad realizes that these two beautiful girls had forgotten what freedom felt like, forgotten who they were created to be, and he starts weeping.

I have to tell you, this image has stuck with me for nearly thirty years. In many ways, isn't their story our story as well? We forget what fullness of life feels like because stagnancy sneaks up on us. We don't realize it's happening until we find ourselves standing in our own crap, scared to leave the comfort of what we know, and malnourished from years of self-contempt.

Because of the nature of my work at MOPS International, I get to travel the world and talk with a lot of women, and everywhere I go I hear the same two things. It doesn't matter where I am—whether it's sitting on the dirt floor of a home in Honduras or in a corner office in New York City. First, women tell me they feel exhausted because they are doing so much. Second, they tell me that they don't feel like they are doing enough with their lives. Exhausted because they are doing so much, and terrified that they aren't doing enough.

We are running around at the pace of Chihuahuas on

cocaine while simultaneously feeling like we are stuck, tired, and lonely. God is stirring our souls, but we can never get to them because we are too busy pinning recipes to our Pinterest boards, which we will never actually use because we don't have time. We are a generation of women who have forgotten what it feels like to be fully alive.

Before we can talk about how to have more fun, it seems to me that we need to figure out how we got here—to the place where we have forgotten to have fun in the first place. I believe it has something to do with three random and seemingly unrelated things: the Puritans, paper cuts, and fake fun.

THE PURITAN WORK ETHIC

America's cultural destiny was set in motion in part by Puritans who left Europe looking for religious freedom. They brought with them a morality rooted in the virtues of hard work, self-discipline, self-reliance, and frugality.

The demands of starting a new society from scratch were no doubt relentless, since there was always more to do. It would have been easy to frown upon having fun when all able-bodied people were desperately needed to meet needs and build a new world. How could one legitimately rationalize taking time to have some fun when one was needed at the plow or in the kitchen? Besides, by doing more, one could feel useful, which would be a reward in and of itself. Fun was also moderated to maintain propriety, caricatured in a famous quote from cultural critic H. L. Mencken, who said Puritanism is "the haunting fear that someone, somewhere may be happy."[1]

If at any point in the last year you have felt lazy or chastised yourself for procrastinating, you are experiencing some vestige of Puritan moralism. If you at some point opted to "do just one more thing," or had vacation time left over at the end of the year because it was just too hard to get away and there would be piles of work waiting for you when you returned, you have lived out the Puritan work ethic firsthand. If you have felt like you shouldn't be enjoying yourself because there are so many other people in the world who are suffering, you are in the club too.

DEATH BY PAPER CUTS

An idea my therapist shared with me has helped me understand why some of us aren't living with joy and gusto, and that's the idea of paper cuts. She explained to me that everyone at some point feels stuck because we pick up things along the way that are too heavy to be holding. Sometimes it is big things like loss or addiction or abuse or secrets that feel too shameful to say out loud, so we just put them on our backs and lug them around for forty years.

But what is more common is what she calls "death by paper cuts." This is when you experience a bunch of little hurts, embarrassments, or disappointments over the years, and you think they shouldn't impact you. But then, one day, you realize that the cumulative effect has created a massive gaping wound that you didn't even notice was there. It isn't until you become aware that you have overwhelming anxiety or exhaustion, or that you have begun to shrink back, or that you have stopped being honest to avoid getting hurt again that you realize that all those small wounds have worn you down to where it feels too tiring or irresponsible to choose fun.

FAKE FUN

Fun is a word that can be deceiving because it can be used to describe the best and worst of human behavior. Bullies who torment others for "fun" or addicts whose "fun" disintegrates relationships might think they are enjoying themselves in the moment, but it is fake fun. We believe we are doing something that should feel enjoyable, but in the end it leaves us feeling more isolated and worse than when we started. If in doubt about what kind of fun to pursue, here are three ways to spot a fake.

You won't regret real fun. Fake fun makes you feel like hell. Unworthy pursuits all have the same wretched aftermath, regret, hangovers, shame, and feeling like you need to keep things secret. Real fun will leave you energized and like the best version of yourself.

Fake fun ignores stress; real fun fixes it. I know a guy who defines fun as smoking pot and playing hours of online gaming. The more work stress he is under, the more pot and gaming he does because he believes it helps him forget the anxiety and responsibilities that are demanding his attention. His stress never gets better, and he lives in an unending cycle of stress and fake fun. Another friend with similar work stress mobilized her colleagues who were all feeling the same way, and they all decided to do CrossFit together at lunch to burn off some steam. She says that they have so much fun laughing together about how hard it is. Not only that, once when they were driving back to the office from class, they figured out a way to distribute work more efficiently so that everyone's stress levels lowered. My proactive friend is having way more fun than the thinly veiled distress-loop of my other buddy.

Fake fun is never satisfied. Healthy fun is typically a renewable pleasure—no matter how many times we do it, it is still enjoyable. For example, if you have a healthy appreciation for food, eating will be fun at every meal. But if you're devouring more than your body needs, you start to need more and more extreme amounts to make food interesting. If you have a voracious demand for more and more expensive toys, kinky sex, online shopping for stuff you don't need or use, achievement at work, and so on, the root of your craving is likely an inner void that will keep demanding more and never be satisfied.

When we wake up and realize that we're wasting time on fake fun, the common mistake is to try to replace bad habits with something we consider to be more virtuous, like exercise or dieting. This doesn't usually work. The only thing that can successfully replace fake fun is real fun.

LOYAL SOLDIER

I have used all these tactics—puritanical reasoning, wounds from paper cuts, and fake fun—to reason with myself about why it was OK that I wasn't having more fun. In some circles of therapy this is called being a loyal soldier to sabotaging thoughts. I call it being not fun to hang out with.

Richard Rohr in his book *Falling Upward* talks about how after World War II some Japanese communities noticed that their returning soldiers were struggling to assimilate back into their everyday lives. Their only identity during their most formative years had been to be loyal soldiers to their country, and the trauma and weight of war were heavy. Now coming home, they needed a new identity that was bigger than war, a more expansive understanding of themselves as wholehearted humans. Rohr explains the action taken to heal their situation:

> The Japanese communities created a communal ritual whereby a soldier was publicly thanked and praised effusively for his service to the people. After this

was done at great length, an elder would stand and announce with authority something to this effect: "The war is now over! The community needs you to let go of what has served you and served us well up to now. The community needs you to return as a man, a citizen, and something beyond a soldier."[2]

There is wisdom in recognizing that most of us need a rite of passage to help us transition from one way of being to another. A simple process, known as discharging your loyal soldier, can help us create closure and instill a new sense of freedom and fullness of life.

Before we can go any further, I want to invite you to discharge your loyal soldier so you can start regaining the lightness of fun. Here is a liturgy that is both prayer and blessing and that can be a powerful tool to thank your loyal soldier for the ways it has showed up to protect you, and then to dismiss it from duty.

God, over the years I have tried to do things right and attempted to be responsible and hardworking. I have employed my loyal soldier well. But it is time for a new season. I bless my loyal soldier for serving me well and now I dismiss it from duty. May my body and soul feel a lightness that whispers of Eden. May fun return to my days not in frivolousness but in fullness of life. And may I invite my family and friends into this same experience of freedom. Let it be so.

Once that soldier has been thanked for its service and sent on its way, you get to start living life as a fun-loving civilian! Yes, you'll still need to buy groceries and drive carpool and clean the occasional toilet. But you no longer have to be bossed around by a rigid commanding officer. Perhaps while you're dutifully gathering kale and quinoa at the grocery store, you dance to the music playing over the loudspeaker as you push your cart down the aisle. Or perhaps on the day you pick up all the neighborhood kids from school, you show up wearing a wig of neon green hair. The win in discharging your loyal soldier is that you are set free to embrace the joy of living again.

I am eight years old, standing in a horse barn in Pennsylvania, and my dad is weeping.

Not being one to linger with his emotions for long, he looks at me and says, "We've got this." Then he creates a plan. He decides that we are going to sleep in the barn for as long as it takes to help these horses remember who they are. He goes out and buys sleeping bags, which we lay in the hayloft. Over the next few days, we bathe the horses, clean out their stalls, and each day my dad feeds them nourishing food by hand, each time leading them a little farther out toward the pasture.

On the third day, the horses had regained much of their strength, and my dad led them out of the barn through the gate and into the pasture. As soon as they crossed through the gate, their ears perked up, and you could see them remembering what fun it was to be out there. They felt the sun on their backs and started running around, bucking, chasing each other, rolling in the dirt, and eating grass. That night we had a hard time getting them back into the barn, because once you remember what fun feels like you never want to go back to standing in your own crap.

This book is your invitation back out into the field.

HONORABLY DISCHARGE YOUR
SOLDIER BY PAINTING IT HOT PINK

Find little plastic army guys at the dollar store, or even a soldier action figure in the toy aisle. Paint it hot pink and then make a cozy little nest for this soldier gal in your underwear drawer. She's done her tour of duty, and seeing her snuggled up in your favorite sock that's lost its mate (Really? It's always the favorites, isn't it?) will remind you that she's off the clock.

SEASONAL FUN

SUMMER: Swim in a river or lake. Don't forget a huge blow-up raft shaped like a swan.

FALL: Rake a huge pile of leaves near the sidewalk and then bury yourself in it until you hear someone passing by. Pop out and scare the living daylights out of them. (If your home has no leaves, rake a neighbor's lawn.)

WINTER: Sled down the biggest hill you can find. If you're sledless, Target sells cafeteria trays as sleds now!

SPRING: Wait for a rainy day and go puddle splashing.

CHAPTER 2

HAVE MORE FUN WITH FRIENDSHIP

There is nothing I would not do for my friends.
I have no notion of loving people by halves,
it is not my nature.

JANE AUSTEN, *NORTHANGER ABBEY*

My friend Jackie is smart, beautiful, incredibly thoughtful, and a total catch. Except that she isn't dating anyone right now for a reason you would never guess even if I gave you a million tries. She emailed me a few weeks ago with the details after I asked about how a date she had scheduled had gone:

> The butt burn is all I've been doing for thirteen days now. Here's how it happened: I was politely sitting on my counter doing an Epsom salt foot bath in the sink with a stock pot of bone broth heating behind me.

About fifteen minutes in, there was a loud bang and my butt was on fire, but my immediate thoughts were of cleaning up the gallon of broth that had spewed across my kitchen floor. About a half hour into cleaning I could no longer stand the pain, and I had to go look at my butt. The entire thing was red as a tomato. I tried to pull my sweats back up, but the pain was so bad, I had to leave them below my cheeks and clean the kitchen with two very red buns hanging out the top of my pants. (Still keeping it classy, like always.)

I have no explanation for the whole business. The only explanation I can think of is that it turned into a pressure cooker and eventually blew. My whole right cheek was covered in blisters at one point. According to the dermatologist I saw yesterday, scabs are forming under the blistered skin. We have to kill the blistered skin to get the scabs out in order for this thing to heal. Fortunately, the killing process is fairly painless— we're just going to drown the injured skin.

My butt is covered in white nonstick gauze that is taped right into the center of my butt cheeks. It's like wearing a really dysfunctional diaper. It hurts like the dickens all the time, and I spend as much time as possible packed in ice. I also had to buy ice packs with straps. (You can read that last sentence again.) Between my diaper and strap-on ice packs, I am super cool right now.

So yeah, not dating anyone at the moment.

Am I the only one with tears streaming down my face? This is a very eligible woman who is sitting at home in a makeshift diaper. Please make it a priority to find friends who will email you about their butt burns. Please also make it a priority to email people about your butt burns, because the best way to cultivate friendship is through shared absurdity.

SHARED ABSURDITY CREATES BONDS

Shared absurdity can happen in a lot of different ways, but it usually starts with choosing to do something unexpected in a pivotal moment and takes on-the-spot thinking along with a commitment to not being embarrassed. It doesn't have to happen often, but when it does, it will bond you for life with the people who experience it alongside you. Super random, right? Let me break it down.

My friend Kate decided that she was going to compete in a duathlon to celebrate her fiftieth birthday. She had never done anything athletic before, not even playing soccer in elementary school, so she wanted to ring in a new decade of life with something that was out of her comfort zone. The duathlon consisted of a swim, followed by a bike ride, culminating in another swim to the finish line. She gave herself a year to train for it and was so determined that she never missed one day of training. On the night before the race, four of her closest friends rented a hotel room near the start of the race so that they could all be there to cheer her on first thing in the morning. Everyone was up at 4:30 a.m., Kate from nerves and her friends from excitement. What Kate didn't know was that her friends had all made outrageous outfits and signs to cheer her on. There was lots of glitter and boas; you know, to make sure she could find them in the crowd.

After eating a quick bite, they all headed down to the harbor where the first leg of the swim began. The race started, and Kate jumped in the water; her friends were there at the transition area just in time to see Kate run out of the water, towel off, and hop on her bike. After the bike ride she was feeling strong and staying on pace; she changed out of her biking shoes and headed to the water for the final swim. This time her friends had positioned themselves on the jetty along the harbor that all the swimmers passed on the way to the finish line. They were near the middle of the swim but close enough to the finish line to see her cross.

Everything was great until ten minutes into the last swim. Kate realized the tide had shifted, and she was swimming against the current. It was taking her twice as long to swim the second leg as it had the first, and she was reaching maximum exhaustion. As her friends saw her struggling, they started yelling and cheering as loud as they could, "You've got this, you can make it!" Exhausted panic filled Kate's eyes as she looked up at them and said, "I can't make it."

At that moment, knowing how important it was for Kate to finish this race, one of her friends flung off her boa and yelled, "Stay there, we're coming in." The rest of them looked at her, and in a split second of understanding they all jumped into the water together. Knowing that if Kate touched anyone she would be immediately disqualified, they didn't physically help her. But the sheer bravado of her friends jumping in the water gave Kate an immediate boost of energy, and she and her friends swam the final leg of the race to the finish line together. Kate will tell you that she will never forget what her friends did that day because shared, absurd experiences stay with us forever.

SHARED ABSURDITY CREATES CONNECTION

Shared absurdity also creates moments of connection. In my life, it always seems to happen when I take something ordinary and add a twist. It typically takes a little extra effort, but not too much.

For example, we have a tradition in our family that whenever a guest leaves our house, we do a running goodbye. We learned it from our friends the Meissners and have now made it our own. Here's what happens: when our guests are piling into their car to drive away, our whole family lines up shoulder to shoulder in our front yard, and we get into a runner's starting position. Then, as they drive down our street, we run alongside them, waving and yelling and making a big scene. You can see our guests shaking their heads and laughing as they round the corner at the end of our street. They may think we're nuts, but it is a moment that lets them know they matter to us.

Another family tradition is that we invite everyone who visits our house to sign their names under our table. Jon Weece, a pastor in Kentucky, first gave us the idea. He said that when people put their name in your home, they feel instantly like they belong. Of course, the most hilarious part of the whole experience is seeing people crawl on the ground under our table. This is also a true test of friendship, because there will for sure be dog hair and crumbs under there. I have to take deep breaths and get over myself to invite them to participate in the first place, but creating small moments of meaning has the power to imprint friendships with an extra level of intimacy and intention that form a foundation of trust.

SHARED ABSURDITY MAKES STRANGERS INTO FRIENDS

Shared absurdity also means being willing to make strangers into friends. This is something I learned from my mom. She is notorious for meeting someone on an airplane, and by the next holiday they are sitting at our table for dinner.

She has never met a stranger who is unworthy of her time, and she has the friends to prove it.

Just by chance a few years ago my mom, Cindy, ended up sitting next to a woman at a concert, and they began to make small talk about the weather. Well, the small talk about the weather turned into small talk about families, which turned into small talk about the fact that this woman, who my mom was meeting for the first time, had cheated on her husband and gotten pregnant from a guy who was in jail. As my mom talked to her, she found out that the woman had no one. Her family had disowned her, she had no friends, and she was so scared that she was going to have to go to the hospital and deliver this baby alone. So my mom tells her, "I'll go with you." And she did. A few months later she held her new friend's hand as she brought her baby into the world.

When my mom told me this story, she said that she has learned over time that God's love is lavish and scandalous and ridiculously inclusive. She said, "After reading about all the messy people who God loved, it became apparent to me that God is not selective about the people he calls friends. And so, I'm not either."

I did not receive this openness with strangers as a genetic hand-me-down from my mom. If I have the choice between getting through emails or chitchatting with my seatmate on a plane, my default would be to choose email every time. But watching my mom and the way she lives her life, I decided that I wanted to be more like Cindy.

Now every time I go to the airport for a trip I ask God for experiences, then I let myself be open to whomever I am going to meet.

When I approach the world with this posture, I am never disappointed with the results. On a recent trip, I met several new friends. The first was Sugan Kumar, who had a massive brain hemorrhage a few years ago. His doctors didn't think he was going to make it, but he did. He is resilient and back at work, doing things that defy what health professionals thought would be possible after such a severe brain bleed. Now we are friends on Facebook, and every once in a while I get a message from him asking how my family is doing. I also exchanged phone numbers with Don and Ethel, who were going to Don's sixtieth class reunion in Ohio. They were worried that all the people at the reunion were going to be old and boring because they still liked to have fun. When they are in Colorado next time, we are going to grab dinner together. Because fun is always a good idea.

Community is such a big buzzword right now. Everyone wants it, and so many people are theorizing about how to create it, but what I want to scream over the noise is that it is already there. We live in communities. The relationships we are longing for are right in front of us, waiting to be noticed. I buy my groceries at the same store every week. My kids get picked up by the same bus driver every morning. I even see some of the same people on my commute every day. What this tells me is that I have opportunities every day to choose relationship wherever I go.

My goal is that when people leave my presence, they feel better about themselves (not better about me). Let me tell you, it is so much more fun. Now I *know* the people in my life. I can tell you about Bo and Jeremiah, who cash us out at our local grocery store, King Soopers. I could tell you what Bo is doing on his day off this week and also when Jeremiah got his haircut last, because he asked my opinion on what style to get. Community is a result of fun that starts with an awkward conversation and turns into friendship.

SHARED ABSURDITY FORCES PEOPLE TO BE IN THE PARADE

In eighth grade, Drea decided that we were going to be friends. I had just moved to town and didn't know anyone, so it sounded like a good idea to me. Twenty years later, I have to tell you: it was the best decision I never made. We couldn't be more different. Drea is bold and unafraid to ask for what she wants. Not to mention, she's fiercely smart and unapologetically herself.

Growing up, she was the rebellious one who tried everything, dated a lot of boys, and lived all over the world, learning languages and making lifelong friends. Wherever she is, things come to life.

She and I toasted my first kiss with chocolate milkshakes at one o'clock in the morning.

We ditched Mr. Thuleen's physics class more times than I am comfortable sharing.

When she confessed to her parents that she got a speeding ticket while ditching school to go shopping with her boyfriend an hour away, she ran away to my house until the storm blew over.

You can see why I love her.

And now, it has been many years since eighth grade, and we are still friends. Mostly because I am convinced that anyone who knew me at thirteen and still wants to spend time with me is someone who I should do everything I can to keep around.

Drea lives in Brooklyn, and I live in Denver, which means that now we rely on airplanes and text messages instead of handwritten notes passed across a classroom. Last summer I took my whole crew to stay with Drea, her hubby, Hal, and their son, Bowie, for a week in New York City. There were eight of us in their two-bedroom Brooklyn apartment, which was glorious and hilarious.

One of my favorite memories from this trip was at the Coney Island Mermaid Parade. The Mermaid Parade is a long-standing tradition in New York, and millions of people attend every year. Drea decided that the best way to culminate our visit was to not watch the parade but to participate in it. My kids and husband were skeptical, but Drea wouldn't take no for an answer. So we grabbed costumes from their costume box and the dollar store near their house. We named ourselves "The Punky Pirates" and set out for Coney Island. Everyone on the subway stared, which my kids found embarrassing but liberating. After departing the train and weaving through the hundreds of thousands of people who had lined the streets to watch, we made it to the holding area where all the floats and participants waited for their turn to begin the parade route. Our number was called, and before we knew it we were walking through the streets of New York, waving to the crowd. My girls loved every minute of it, and even my fifteen-year-old son said it was something he would never forget.

As Drea and I walked with the crowd of mermaids and pirates that day, all I could think about was how Drea *does* things. I want to be around people who do things. I want to be around people who dream big and walk in parades and go first by making crazy suggestions. I don't want to be around people who judge or talk about what others do. For twenty years, Drea has been showing me how to live with freedom and fun, and she also frequently reminds me to take advantage of any opportunity to wear a costume.

SHARED ABSURDITY AFFIRMS DIFFERENT OPINIONS

If at any point you feel like your relationships are suffering because of judgment or comparison, take Amy Poehler's advice: "I have many friends who have had natural child-birth, I applaud them. I have friends who have used dou-las and birthing balls and pushed babies out in tubs and taxicabs. I have a friend who had two babies at home! In bed! Her name is Maya Rudolph, she is baby champion, and she pushed her cuties out *Little House on the Prairie* style! Good for her! Not for me. This is the motto women should constantly repeat over and over again. Good for her! Not for me."[1]

What a brilliant and grounding mantra, right? There are countless ways to live and even more ways to parent. Instead of feeling like we need to analyze everyone else's decisions, we can choose to say, "Good for her! Not for me." Brilliant.

SHARED ABSURDITY MEANS DING-DONG DITCHING YOUR NEIGHBORS

Two weeks after we moved into our current home, my girls—who were six and eight at the time—were out in the front yard, coloring pictures and writing cute messages on them. Being new to the neighborhood, we were trying to get the lay of the land, and right next door to us is a house we refer to as "the pink house." None of the neighbors knew who lived there, and the blinds were always closed. There were never trash cans out front, and the car never moved, so we figured either no one lived there or they were away on an extended trip.

After finishing their pictures, my girls came over to me and said, "Mom, we want to ding-dong ditch our neighbors and leave our notes by their doors." We had only lived there for two weeks, and we were already the loudest family on the street—music playing, kids fighting, and every light in the house on at night. The last thing we needed was to make more of a scene. But I was determined to have more fun, so I pointed to five houses on the street that they could ding-dong ditch. Not coincidentally, they were the five houses where I knew no one was home, including the pink house. The girls ran down the street, ringing doorbells, leaving notes, hiding in the bushes, and generally being hilarious.

The pink house was the last house on their list. They rang the doorbell. No answer, just like I had planned. That is, until two minutes later when the door creaked open and an elderly woman in a nightgown looked down, picked up the note, read it, and burst into tears. At this point I am like, *Great, the Ariotos move in and are already annoying our neighbors.* Then, she turned around and slammed her door shut. The girls were stunned and ran home embarrassed, feeling terrible that they made this woman cry. I reassured them that it was going to be fine, and told them I would go over to her house the next day to sort everything out. After the girls went inside, I contemplated the possible scenarios. Was she angry that the kids were ding-dong ditching her? Was she unstable?

Joe and I ended up taking the kids out for dinner to

distract them, because feelings run big in our family. But when we got home later that night, there was a plate of store-bought cookies on our front porch with a note that said:

> Hello, new family,
>
> I live in the pink house next to you. I have to let you know that I have been housebound for the last two months, and I haven't seen anyone in that time because my family lives far away and haven't been able to visit. I have been praying that God would send someone to me to let me know he still loves me. When I picked up the note your girls left, I couldn't believe what it said.
>
> Thank you, thank you, thank you.

At this point, I turned to my girls and asked what their note had said. They both looked at me and said, "You are lovable."

You are lovable.

Stay there; we're coming in.

Don't miss any opportunity to wear a costume, because ...

I'll go with you, and don't you dare worry about wearing a diaper.

These are the shared absurdities of friendship. May you use them to have the most fun you have ever had with friends, old and new.

The thing about shared absurdity is that it needs to be

shared. You might share absurdity with a blistered-butt friend you've known for ages, or you might be walking in a parade with strangers dressed like mermaids. It might require you to ask someone their name. When you use it, you communicate to them that they matter. If you're not in the habit, it's not difficult at all. There are literally three words: "What's your name?" See how easy that is? Then use it.

PLAN AN UNEXPECTED BIRTHDAY PARTY FOR YOURSELF OR A FRIEND

1. Celebrate it at the roller rink, dressed in disco gear
2. Recreate prom from the year you were born
3. Host a stargazing party and serve s'mores
4. Hold it at a video-game arcade (no, actually, that sounds horrible)
5. At a trampoline park
6. Wearing superhero costumes out to your favorite restaurant
7. With a DJ, dancing your buns off
8. With a clown or a balloon artist

CHAPTER 3

HAVE MORE FUN WITH PARENTING

> When you're a twerking mother, balance is really important because you don't want to go too low and blow out your butt and bust your knee.
>
> AMY POEHLER

There are so many things about motherhood that have surprised me. Like the fact that no one told me I would give birth to a placenta. I also wasn't aware that if you get the flu as a mom, you basically just continue living your life . . . but you do it throwing up. Nothing changes. True story: I was throwing up in the bathroom, thanks to a particularly persistent flu, when my young kids came in and whispered, "Mom are you OK? Also, what's for dinner?"

My own mom recently surprised me with her mothering skills when she called me the morning of the solar eclipse last year and reminded me not to look directly at the sun. I am an almost forty-year-old woman, but my mom made a point to call me on her way to work just to make sure my eyes would be safe. She can't help herself. Because once someone calls you mom, whether by birth or adoption, you are destined for the rest of your life to worry about their eyes during an eclipse. Yet another surprise about being a mom.

I have also been pleasantly surprised as a mom by my ability to know stuff. I wasn't aware that, as a mother of three kids, one of the super-abilities I would develop is "finding all the things." *Mom, where's the left blue Barbie shoe? Under the bathroom sink, inside the plastic Tupperware container you used as a pool so Barbie could practice her synchronized swimming skills last week. You're welcome.* That is some next-level mothering right there.

Perhaps my most startling realization is that moms are the ultimate of everything. That is actually a fact. How do I know this? Because what word do people use to define the highest of anything? "Mother . . . ." The mother of all storms, the mother of all traffic, the mother lode. To be a mother is to be a force of nature.

It can take a lot of concentrated effort to be a force of nature, and sometimes you have all that energy and feel like you are killing it. If that is you right now, then all I have to say is please teach us your ways.

There might be other times when you feel like your days have turned into a run-on sentence, and chronic, low-grade mom guilt is the soundtrack of your life. The responsibilities and needs are never-ending, and you discover yourself in the isolation of your own home, finding all the lost things, doing the most surprising work you have ever done.

It is in these moments of existential crisis that you need a trusted friend to remind you of the motto that might just be able to reframe your entire parenting perspective. Occasionally, after you push a baby out of your womb, well-meaning women in the grocery store will peer longingly at your precious offspring and implore you to "treasure every minute." This is not helpful. Do not adopt this mantra. I would never utter such an inane suggestion, because I have kids. In fact, I am parenting children at this very moment. The last sentence was written while I simultaneously yelled down the hall to tell my ten-year-old to clean her bunny's cage because it smells like a barn in her room.

The mantra that has changed everything about parenting for me is "have more fun." Raising kids is some of the most important work we will do, and it can be some of the most joyful work if we choose to let it be. Just for the record, "have more fun" is different than "treasure every moment." If "treasure every moment" is a precious faith-based film that makes everyone feel a little guilty, then "have more fun" is an endearing, gritty, and hilarious PG-13 flick that your kids will tell stories about when they are adults. I know this for a fact, thanks to my own parents who utilized a "have more fun" parenting style, and I turned out to be fairly well-adjusted.

THE FOUR COMPONENTS OF "HAVE MORE FUN" PARENTING

Parenting is one of the coolest and most invigorating opportunities we have as human beings. We are the ones who will set the stage for most of what our kids believe about themselves and the world for the rest of their lives. While this is a weighty endeavor, it doesn't have to be all chore charts, no sleep, and frustration.

Mothering Can Be Fun

Hot take: mothering can be fun. It's amazing what can happen when you start by *assuming* this rather than the alternative. The narrative we hear over and over is that being a mom is hard and exhausting. I am here to challenge that assumption. What if it was invigorating, transformative, and the most fun work we will ever do?

My friend Cathy is an awesome mom to three grown boys. When I asked for her secret to raising well-adjusted, thriving kids, she said that it all started with how she viewed motherhood. Because her mom believed that mothering could be fun, Cathy parented with the same expectation. Her beliefs shaped her behavior, which in turn impacted her kids.

Here is a fact that you probably already know from experience—and a lesson I have learned the hard way more times than I care to admit: as a mom, your attitude matters more than everyone else's. Your attitude determines the climate of your entire home, and there is no getting around it. All eyes are looking to you, watching for clues, absorbing your vibes, and modeling your attitude. This is the responsibility of motherhood: to inject a positive attitude, be willing to diffuse the tension, and make it OK to think about problems proactively. If you don't do it, who else will?

If you are having fun, everyone in your house will as well. Ever wonder how generational blessing trickles down in families? All it takes is one mom who is committed to wholeness and joy. Her kids will have that same perspective, and eventually they will parent with the same wholeness and joy. This is powerful stuff. You are the person who can change the things that bother you about your family culture. You are the person who can break cyclical patterns, and you are the person who can bring fun and lightness into not only your home but into your lineage for generations to come. It is generational legacy, and it can start with you.

Choose to Enjoy Your Kids

I recently heard an audiobook about parenting called *Launching Rockets* that touched on this concept, and it has revolutionized how I mother my kids. Here is the idea:

What if our first responsibility in raising kids is to enjoy them? Typically most people believe their first responsibility in parenting is to raise kids to be productive adults. But what if that is second, and our first responsibility is to enjoy them? Why is this so important? Because kids have incredibly sensitive radars. They pick up very early on whether their parents enjoy them or if they simply tolerate them. This is important, because it shapes how a kid sees the world for the rest of their lives.

The other reason why choosing to enjoy our children is important is because kids are just not very enjoyable to raise at times. It might be that their personality clashes with ours, or that there are very real physical or emotional issues. Or it could be they are transitioning into a new phase of development and stumbling as they exert newly found freedom. Whatever it is, sometimes a kid is just hard. But with that kid, at that time, it is more important than ever that you do everything you can to find *something*, however small or trivial, that you enjoy about them. Here is a direct quote that struck me right in the gut: "If you have a kid who is making you miserable, that kid is miserable."[1]

Remember: the thing that is frustrating you right now about your child will, at some point down the road, frustrate you for the exact opposite reason. When your child is a newborn and isn't sleeping through the night, it makes you insane. But when that same child is a sophomore in high school and sleeping at 1:22 p.m. on a Saturday afternoon, you are going to be frustrated. When your three-year-old won't stop talking or asking questions, it can drive you crazy. But eventually you'll be commiserating about your teenager with your friends, saying, "I just wish she would talk to me." Whatever it is now, whatever is annoying you or making you crazy about being the parent of this particular child, at some point in the future it will probably be something else. So maybe choose to enjoy this moment and not hold the frustrations so tightly.

It is a massive responsibility to raise a kid, and that is why you need the lightness of joy that comes from surrendering expectations and focusing on what is going right. Communicating what we appreciate about our kids helps them to feel deeply known and loved. And this parenting posture is a heck of a lot more fun than constantly feeling frustrated and exhausted.

If you do have a child who is difficult to enjoy, try shifting your thoughts. Maybe that starts with a quick prayer like "God, please show me something about this child that I haven't seen before." Most of the time when we do this, it changes something in us, and that in turn changes something in them.

Respond with the Unexpected

On school mornings, my husband and I take turns dropping our children off at the bus stop. With three kids at three different schools, all with different bus pick-up times, we have a rather robust morning routine. Our son

Joseph, now a sophomore, is counting down the days until he gets his driver's license, because having your parents drop you off at the bus stop is not cool. (Or so I am told.) I am also told that my bus drop-off practices are excessive.

On my drop-off days, I drive to the stop, pull up to the curb, put the car in park, open my door, and walk around to his side of the car to give him a big hug and a kiss on the cheek before he heads off to school. One morning, as I pulled away from the curb, a text popped up on my phone from my son. All it said was:

"Mom, you are invading my personal space."

I stared at it for a minute, my eyes stinging as I vacillated between being hurt and being angry.

So I texted back:

"You came out of my personal space."

"P.S. Moms can hug their kids whenever they want. Xoxo. Have a great day."

After that, we texted funny emojis and then later that night, after he shared that he was probably scarred for life by that visual but admitted it made him laugh, we came to a truce. I agreed to hug and kiss him before we got in the car to spare him the embarrassment of the bus stop scene.

So much of parenting is me making the choice to not get my feelings hurt and to choose lightheartedness instead. I could have reprimanded my son for his snarky comment, and I could have gotten frustrated that he didn't appreciate how much I love him. Instead I chose fun, and while I don't always make the right decision in the moment, it pays off big time when I do. Fun disarms frustration and changes the script we are expecting to hear; it helps us avoid ruts and opens up trust and communication, especially with our teens. Of course, there are times for meaningful conversation where we let our kids know they have hurt our feelings by being rude or disrespectful, but overall my experience has been that fun dissipates annoyance and opens lines of communication faster than any other method.

This same tactic works for toddlers as well as teens. One of my kids had a tendency to melt down if we ran errands too far past her naptime. One day we were at the mall, shopping for a flower-girl dress for a wedding she was going to be in, and after a few stores she had reached her max. She melted down with flailing arms and loud cries between a rack of wedding dresses and a display of bedazzled shoes. I scooped her up, grabbed my purse, abandoned our shopping objectives, and held her so close that her ear was near my lips.

As she cried, I started whispering all the things I love about her. "I love how well you take care of your pets. I love how you twirl your blankie in your hand so it lays just right when you fall asleep. I love that you are so brave climbing things at the playground. I love how your laugh lights up the room. . . ." Within fifteen seconds, her crying and flailing had stopped, and she was listening intently to what I was saying.

To be clear, this is the highlight reel of my parenting.

I frequently choose the less effective and less fun route, but what I am reminded of over and over again is that owning the moment by doing the unexpected can be a life-changing gift to our kids . . . and ourselves.

INITIATE THE JEDI STRATEGY
OF FUN PARENTING

The best way to have thriving kids is to be a thriving parent. I can't tell you the number of parents I talk to (moms, I'm looking at you) who are slowly withering away inside because they have become martyrs for the sake of feeling like a good parent. They don't take the class they have been longing to try because someone else would have to pick up their kids from practice, so instead they seethe inside while waiting at the practice field for an hour. This is why it is important to differentiate between *sacrificing* and *settling*. For parents, sacrificing comes with the job. It is the daily practice of putting other people's needs ahead of your own, it is giving your kid the last piece of pie, it is cleaning up throw-up in the middle of the night, and it is a remarkably centering and expanding privilege that comes with parenting. Sacrifice makes us better human beings.

Settling, on the other hand, makes us exhausted, resentful, cynical, and apathetic. Settling is choosing to live in a house you can barely afford and staying at the job you hate to live there. It means not taking the class that will revive your soul, because your kids would have to figure out dinner on their own. It is the secret belief that your best days are behind you, so you don't take care of your body because "hurting is just part of getting older." You don't take your vacation days because there is always too much work. You feel apathetic about your marriage—and your kids know it—but it feels exhausting, expensive, and risky to start marriage counseling.

Settling is resignation. Sacrifice is holy offering.

Here are a few questions to help recalibrate. Do your kids know what your dreams are? Do they see you pursuing them? How will your kids learn to pursue their dreams if they don't have an example? Are you brave enough to face your darkness and unresolved fears so that they don't spill over onto your kids (and then they will have to go to therapy in fifteen years to sort out the things you could have dealt with right now)? When we actively take responsibility for our own flourishing, it spills over onto the people around us. Our kids benefit, our spouses benefit, and we begin to live in more dynamic and energizing ways.

One of the best ways to have more fun with parenting is to look at other parents who are having fun. This isn't playing the comparison game, it is gleaning inspiration, like you would from a brilliant musician or a talented artist. It is watching how they work their craft and then finding your own groove with it.

Take my friend Hank Fortener, father to two little girls

and husband to a beautiful wife. He leads an organization called Adopt Together, which is basically a kick-starter to help families fund adoptions. He is masterful at creating memorable moments and flipping the script to live in unexpected ways.

A few years ago, when his girls were little and his wife was deep in the motherhood trenches, he saw how complex and beautiful and important this mothering gig is. In response, he started slow clapping for moms he would see out in public. If he saw a mom loading up groceries and kids into her car, he would stop and give her a slow clap and say, "Well done, this is impressive work you are doing. You deserve a round of applause." He does this because moms are a force of nature who occasionally could benefit from an unexpected round of applause.[2]

So go out into the world today and slow clap for the next mom you see, because we are in it together and this is going to be fun.

Here are some of the best ideas I have gleaned from the fun moms (and dads) I know.

Make a Morning-Routine Playlist. *My friend Erin taught me this.* This idea has saved us a lot of yelling and tears over the years. Instead of reminding the kids to brush their teeth or put shoes on, a simple solution is to make a playlist where each song cues them to transition to the next activity. My kids know that when "This Is My Year" by Family Force 5 comes on, it means that they should be getting dressed. When "Glorious" by Macklemore (the clean version, deep breaths) comes on, they should be eating breakfast. It takes a few days for all of us to get into our groove, and we regularly make a new playlist when we get tired of the songs, but overall my kids love starting their day with their favorite songs, and I love not having to nag.

Write the Kids Notes. *My neighbor Ruth taught me this.* Every few months I try to remind my kids that they are seen in all their uniqueness, so I do random things like write a personalized "top ten things I love about you" list with quirky, specific examples. I print them out and put them on their breakfast plate or in their lunch box. They usually open it, read it quickly, and joke with me about how they already know I love them. But without fail, a few weeks later when I think the letters have been crumpled up and thrown away, I find their lists tucked under their pillow or taped on the wall behind their door, or I walk by their room and catch them reading them, because we all need someone to go out of their way to remind us that we are seen and loved.

Climb Something. *My friend Alicia taught me this.* I've noticed that kids don't like to go outside and play as much as they did in the past. A lot of the kids in our neighborhood are so busy that unstructured play after school isn't even an option, not to mention the rising rates of stress and anxiety in kids as young as six. Ten years ago, the word *stress* was not part of our childhood vernacular. But a great way to retrain our kids is to go outside with them and climb something. When is the last time you climbed a tree? Or got a ladder out and sat on the roof of your house to look at the stars. We are all longing for freedom, respect, adventure, and someone to say, "I believe in you." One of the best ways to provide those feelings for ourselves is to do something out of the ordinary, outside our comfort zones.

Say Yes. *My father-in-law, Ed, taught me this.* One of the most powerful phrases I have ever witnessed a parent tell their kids is, "I will always try to say yes." This changed the parent-child dynamic, because their kid trusted that their parent was trying to say yes. If they said no, there was a good reason. It also meant that the parent is intentionally choosing to say yes to things their gut might normally have said no to.

Bear Hugs. *My child's Sunday school teacher, Terry, taught me this.* I have learned that when our kids get older and stop climbing in our laps to snuggle, they still need those snuggles even if they're embarrassed to ask for them. So, create nonthreatening opportunities for hugs. If there is competition involved, it really takes it up a notch in the fun department. In our family, we have bear-hug competitions. Everyone bear-hugs each member of the family to see who hugs the hardest. We laugh, and I always lose (thanks, T. rex arms).

Record the Funny Bits. *My friend Margot taught me this.* You know how when your kid says something hilarious, usually by accident, you tell the next adult you see and swear you'll never forget it? And then three hours later you've forgotten it? Write. It. Down. It's not like you have to paint it onto a parchment scroll or chisel it into a block of marble. It's as easy as creating a note on your phone or sending yourself an email. In a few years this will be one of your kid's most treasured memorabilia.

WAYS TO HAVE MORE FUN
WITH PARENTING

Enjoy Your Child

1. On the day you're all already running late for school, go ahead and swing through a fast-food restaurant for pancakes.
2. Leave a love note in your child's shoes.
3. When you're at the park, instead of just watching your child play, climb to the top of the slide and zip down with them.
4. Just once, instead of serving a healthy dinner, pour everyone a bowl of high-sugar, high-color, low-nutrition cereal for dinner. With chocolate milk. Your kids will remember it when they are eighty.
5. Buy a tiny dollar-store surprise and hide it in your child's pillowcase.

CHAPTER 4

HAVE MORE FUN IN YOUR BODY

I got to thinking . . . about all those women on
the Titanic who passed up dessert.

ERMA BOMBECK

M y friend Bridget once received seventy-three texts
from random strangers. They saw a post on craigslist
and wanted to buy a set of *Sweatin' to the Oldies* exercise
DVDs that were made in 1990, featured Richard Simmons,
and were for sale at the bargain price of forty dollars for
the set (what?!). The only problem was, she had no clue
what they were talking about and consequently had to
deal with seventy-three people who were extremely upset
when she texted them back with the news that she didn't
have any exercise videos for sale. After doing some recon,
she figured out that someone had accidentally transposed
a six and an eight when typing their phone number in

their craigslist post and ended up sending the interested customers to Bridget's phone instead of their own.

I have two questions about this situation. First, who knew that Richard Simmons was still in such high demand? Second, is there a secret underground movement of hipsters who are sweating to the oldies? This is the only reasonable conclusion I can come up with to make sense of this situation: that the new ironic and quirky thing to do on a Friday night is to meet up at a refurbished warehouse downtown, wearing mom jeans and high and tight haircuts in order to sweat to the oldies together in a clever and cool way. Please tell me I am right, and please invite me next time it happens.

We human beings are fickle with our fashion, exercise, and beauty trends. The things that are perfectly normal to one generation become appalling or ironic to the next. Like the fact that doctors used to have bowls of cigarettes on their desks to pass out to patients. Or from 1898 to 1910, the Bayer pharmaceutical company sold a very popular cough suppressant made from diacetylmorphine, also known as heroin. No wonder it was so popular.

This fact is why we don't have a microwave in our house. I am convinced we are going to find out at some point that it does weird things to our food. Please don't email me; I know there is all sorts of research that proves otherwise. Just let me live with my absurd beliefs.

I also wonder what beauty trends we participate in now that our grandkids will look back on as barbaric or startling (I am looking at you, Botox). The ancient practice of foot binding in China lasted for over one thousand years and is considered the most dangerous fashion trend in history. Upper-class women had their feet bound because tiny feet were considered attractive to men; if they didn't do it, no man would marry them. Also, it meant women were utterly dependent; they could barely walk after their feet were bound. It took centuries of protest and (finally) a government edict to keep women from binding their daughters' feet. Women were willing to cripple themselves for the sake of being considered beautiful.

Many of the women later regretted practicing the tradition. However, Zhou Guizhen, an old Chinese woman who was among the last women in China with bound feet, in an interview for NPR.org said, "I can't dance, I can't move properly. I regret it a lot. But at the time, if you didn't bind your feet, no one would marry you."[1]

The disorienting truth is that this kind of self-mutilation happens to this day, as the stats on female genital mutilation attest. Older women typically initiate the practice on younger women, and carrying out the cutting is considered a source of honor. Our cosmetic procedures may not be nearly as brutal, but the way we spend our time and our dollars may one day strike us as appalling.

What if we are the generation of women who change this vicious cycle? What if we are the ones who start appreciating our bodies and cease the search for the makeup product or beauty procedure that is going to change our lives? (Hint: It doesn't exist.) I read a quote by Elizabeth Gilbert where she said, "Be the weirdo who dares to enjoy."[2] So few people really enjoy their bodies that it is almost strange to see someone who does. Let's be a new generation of women who are the weirdos who dare to enjoy our bodies and leave a legacy for the girls behind us to do the same.

The first way that we can start enjoying is to start at ground zero by asking the question, "Is my body trying to tell me something?"

The body is often the first to know when we are carrying undue stress, especially when it's not being counterbalanced with care. If we take a few moments to check in with our bodies—notice our breathing, notice where we are carrying tension—then we can get an accurate accounting of how we're really doing and the toll our routines are taking on our precious skin and bones.

Are my shoulders up by my ears?

Am I craving something?

I noticed recently that in every photo I saw of myself that my eyes looked tired. I thought back to the pace of my life and realized I was running on autopilot. The light had gone out behind my eyes, and these two lines from a David Whyte poem came to mind:

When your eyes are tired
the world is tired also.[3]

When our eyes have lost the light, the world tends to lose its light as well. A shadow is cast over our insides and our outsides. I don't want to go through life with tired eyes. I want to go through life with starry eyes—eyes filled with wonder, awe, hope, and curiosity. I call this living lit.

LIVING LIT

Living lit means you feel a sense of your own aliveness; you feel connected to God; your native enthusiasm is intact; you feel joy; you are the instigator of fun. That doesn't mean there aren't challenges. But you know that when obstacles come your way you can handle them.

When a woman is having fun, you can see it on her face. Her inner light is lit. She isn't numb or shut down; she is boldly alive—you might even say radiant. Have you ever met a woman like this? She might be tall or short, a decade past puberty or pushing a century, wrinkly or glowy. But you notice that there's something unique about the way she lives in her skin. The French have a phrase for this, *bien dans sa peau*, literally translated as "well in one's skin," and it is a state everyone notices.

When a woman's light is on, and she is *bien dans sa peau*, she is approachable, she is open, and people want to be around her—she's magnetic. Instead of being preoccupied with herself and her flaws, she can be fully present to others. When she walks in the room, no matter what she is wearing she glows with a sense of inner amusement. She is confident and humble at the same time. Her eyes have life in them.

On the other hand, when a woman's eyes have gone dim, you can see that too. Her eyes look weary, she is closed off, and she is possibly hard to be around. She might feel jealous of other women, be overly critical, or completely retreat and make herself small and quiet so as never to stand out.

There are lots of very good reasons why the light behind our eyes fades. Maybe your husband hasn't looked at you with longing in his eyes for a really long time. Perhaps you have felt inadequate ever since you were a kid, or you feel passed over and undervalued at work. Maybe you are so busy taking care of other people that you've not had time to fuel your own lantern. I get that. No shame. But now is the time to notice it and start living lit.

HOW TO LIGHT YOUR FIRE:
DO IT ANYWAY

Some of us have accepted the belief that the most essential thing about us is that we are flawed and that until we become unflawed, we can't do all the things we'd like to do. I know a woman who didn't wear shorts for forty years because she didn't like her knees. She didn't swim with her kids, didn't know what it felt like to have the warm sun on her legs, and would only make love to her husband in the dark—all because she couldn't get over her perfectly normal knees. This kind of decision-making is why I literally cheered out loud when I read an Instagram post by

@kristineneeley who made the exact opposite decision. She shared a photo of herself with medals around her neck after completing a half marathon and wrote this:

1 year of dreaming. 9 months of planning. 4 months of training. 3 days of run-walk-running 22.4 miles . . . and most importantly, 100% freedom from body shame, eating disorders, and disordered eating and exercise.

This last year and some change, I finally gave up holding onto the last remaining threads of belief in the lie that life is only worth living fully at some ideal weight or that any measure of love was missing from my life because I wasn't there, wherever that nebulous "there" even is.

It's just not true.

Not for me.

Not for you.

Not for any of us.

This body, imperfect as it is, takes me places I could only dream of going and is the beautifully broken and loved vessel of a soul so overwhelmed by the beauty not just of the world around her, but the incredible people in it (you!) and the One who made it all.[4]

Here is the motto I want you to embrace anytime you start talking yourself out of doing something fun because you think your body isn't perfect: Do it anyway.

"I would love to play in the ocean with my kid, but I don't feel confident in a bathing suit." Do it anyway.

"I have always wanted to take a ballroom dance class, but I don't think I am coordinated enough." Do it anyway.

"I really want to go camping with friends but don't want anyone to see me without makeup on." Do it anyway.

Do it anyway and say thank you to your body for the amazing things it does on a daily basis. Thank you to your eyes for getting to witness your kids blowing out their birthday candles, and thank you to your nose for appreciating the smell in the air after it rains. Thank you to your hands for making delicious meals and your arms for holding babies.

COME AND HAVE BREAKFAST

A few years ago, I started seeing a therapist because life caught up with me and I needed some outside perspective to help me sort out the loss, grief, and resulting debilitating anxiety I was dealing with. At the end of our first session, after I told her all the things that were feeling too heavy to carry around any longer, she explained to me that the first step in regaining fullness of life is to eat.

At which point I started questioning whether this was legit therapy or not.

Then the therapist, noticing my doubt, clarified her suggestion. She said that eating was a concept that comes straight from Jesus and how he offered healing, hope, and restoration to people he encountered.

In the Gospel of Mark, Jesus visits a town where there is a leader named Jairus. When Jairus sees Jesus, he falls to his knees before him, begging Jesus to come and heal his daughter because she is about to die. Jesus agrees to go with him, but as they make their way to Jairus's house a crowd gathers. Jesus heals someone else, but before they make it to Jairus's house, one of his servants comes and tells him not to bother bringing Jesus. His daughter is already dead.

Jesus overhears their conversation and insists on going anyway. When they walk in the door, there are people everywhere. They have brought casseroles and cards because it is all we know to do when sad things happen. Jesus tells everyone to leave and takes Jairus and his wife into their daughter's room. Then he takes the girl's hand and whispers over her, *Talitha koum*, which means, "Little girl, get up." (Yep, chills.) At that, she was up and walking around! Then Jesus said, "Give her something to eat."[5]

"Give her something to eat." That happens to be my favorite verse in the whole Bible. In fact, it is my life verse. I believe it translates from the Greek as, "Give her gelato and freshly baked sourdough bread." But my Greek is a little rusty, so I'm not certain.

For Jesus, food was one way he restored fullness of life.

After Jesus was crucified, his friends were devastated and confused. After sticking around in Jerusalem for a little while, they realized that it was time to go back to their day jobs as fishermen. All hope that Jesus was going to make all things right was forgotten. Now all they could think about was whether they were going to catch enough fish to pay the bills. So they go out on the sea at night, but end up catching nothing.

As they are pulling their boat up onto shore, defeated and fishless, they hear a voice from shore suggest that they try casting their nets on the other side of the boat. So, they do. Their nets become so full of fish that they worry about their boats sinking. It is déjà vu, the exact same scenario from when they first met Jesus. Recognizing this, Peter, who is notorious for jumping in water when Jesus is around, swims to shore. As they all arrive on the beach and discover Jesus, their beloved cook has a charcoal fire burning and is preparing a breakfast of grilled fish and warm bread. "Come and have breakfast," he says to his weary disciples.[6]

Come and have breakfast.

Get her something to eat.

Jesus reminds us that to come alive and restore our bodies and souls, the first step is to nourish ourselves, and the second is to take a nap.

TWO NAPS

There is this guy named Elijah who was a man of faith and did awesome things for God. He prayed that it wouldn't rain for three and a half years, and it didn't rain. He also raised a kid from the dead. Well, the people of Israel were starting to be wooed by the false god of their neighbors, Baal. So, Elijah challenged 450 of Baal's prophets to a duel to see who the one true God was. Without using a match, whichever group was able to light an altar with fire first would win. The prophets of Baal were dancing and cutting themselves for hours, trying to summon their god to send fire. Elijah prays once (after dumping loads of water on his kindling) and Yahweh, the one true God, consumes everything with fire. Elijah wins, gets the whole nation of Israel to fall on their faces in repentance, then prays seven times and gets rain back after three and a half years. Then he runs a marathon to the next city he is going to visit.

When Jezebel, the Baal-worshiping queen of the nation he just ran a marathon to, hears that Elijah just defeated and killed 450 of Baal's prophets, she is pissed and threatens to kill Elijah.

Even though he has done all these fantastic things, this threat from the queen rattles Elijah so much so that he runs off into the wilderness, falls under a bush, and tells God that he has had enough. He can't take it anymore. He is doubting his ability and doubting that he has done anything significant. He's ready to tap out.

And here is the thing—Elijah is a guy who has done awesome stuff. But at that moment, he feels like he can't keep up. He wasn't a failure or a hypocrite. He was simply tired.

Here is how I know this: Scripture says that after he had a heart-to-heart with God, he fell asleep.

Then after resting for a while, an angel woke him and said, "Get up and eat." He looked around, and there was some freshly baked bread and a jar of water. He ate and drank and then lay down again. The angel came back a second time and touched him and said, "Get up and eat." So he got up and ate and drank. Strengthened by that food and rest, he went back to doing his thing with confidence.[7]

This guy was exhausted and feeling stuck and questioning everything about his life. And God's amazing spiritual answer to revive him is two naps, two meals. We're good to go. (Which surprisingly sounds a lot like the advice I give to my kids: have a snack and take a nap.)

In a culture that's persuaded us to be unkind to our bodies—belittling them, altering them, reducing them, and carving them up—God is so much kinder and more gracious to our bodies than we are. Take a guilt-free nap today; it's biblical.

BE SURPRISINGLY FIT

I haven't stepped on a scale in over ten years because I couldn't care less what I weigh. What matters to me is that I feel strong (read that as: can carry all the groceries in without having to make two trips), have good cardiovascular endurance, and can physically do all the things I want to do (read that as: cartwheels, kayaking, and general merriment). When I was in college, a dear friend who was fifty years more advanced than me shared with me that her goal in life was to be surprisingly fit. Fit to her had no correlation to thin or free from cellulite. Fit to her meant able to have fun and do cool stuff with her body because she was strong, healthy, and agile. She wanted to surprise people, especially as she got older, with what she was capable of doing. I want the same thing, to be so surprisingly fit that there isn't anything I can't do. Fit equals more fun.

Not only does being strong and agile provide opportunities to get out there and live life to the fullest, exercise is also one of the best antidepressants available. Exercising three to five times a week for at least forty-five minutes had better results for lessening the symptoms of depression than taking Zoloft.[8] Sometimes it can be hard to get started regaining our fitness levels when we feel overwhelmed and exhausted, but the counterintuitive truth is that exercising will give you more energy (true story, I have experienced this firsthand). So get to it and work on becoming surprisingly fit. My go-to way to fit in more exercise is to hop on YouTube and find a quick workout video. There are so many options. Barre, Pilates, CrossFit, it is all there. For free!

START GROWING YOUNG

Thankfully, living lit doesn't depend on our age. Many of us who have known no other culture than the blatantly ageist American one have swallowed the lie that to be youthful is to be worthy and to age is to become less valuable. While other cultures value the gifts that older people offer, we've been conditioned to believe that we're losing, not winning, as we age. How we age is tied up in socialization. We are assigned phases of life, and within those stages there are prescribed psychological, emotional, physical, and financial milestones each step of the way. We blindly follow this consumptive path. If we veer off, we are ostracized by others and ourselves.

Imagine if we grew up hearing stories of how we were going to grow young instead of "preparing for growing old." Can you imagine how much sweeter life would be if we poured those resources into living and celebrating the life we were made to live? I recently read a comment from a woman who is living the way I want to live when I'm her age:

> I'm ninety, but I feel like I am fifty. I don't take any medicine. I never complain. I'm just happy to be alive. I tell people: "Start with what you have, not what you want." Every day I dance for two hours. And I'm still really interesting too. I love politics and literature. I love the sciences. And I've got a boyfriend named Alexander. We exchange books. I don't even know how old he is.[9]

She's dreamy, right? This gal, entirely unconcerned with the arbitrariness of marking age with numbers, is living lit. She's not alone; there are examples of women growing young all around us. Liz Bevington is eighty-seven and known as the skateboarding mama of Venice Beach and is still rollerblading the boardwalk. My mom is sixty-eight, can still do handstands, and kicks butt at her 6:00 a.m. CrossFit class.

Given our culture's crazy posture toward bodies and aging, I hope you're willing to consider what it might look like to choose to grow young in the body you've been assigned, for as many years as you've got it.

SEVEN BEAUTY TRENDS THAT SEEMED LIKE A GREAT IDEA AT THE TIME

1. Gauges (the earrings)
2. Face tattoos
3. Butt implants
4. Leg lengthening
5. Surgical eye-rounding
6. Skin lightening
7. Botox (too soon? Maybe . . .)

Men can be weird about their bodies too. NASA had to relabel the men's sleeve for urinating in space suits from "small, medium, and large" to "large, gigantic, and humungous" because astronauts would only choose the large, and they kept slipping off.

CHAPTER 5

HAVE MORE FUN WITH SEX AND MARRIAGE

A happy marriage is a long conversation which always seems too short.

ANDRE MAROIS

I like to keep things interesting in my marriage, but sometimes those efforts make it a little too interesting. A few years ago, our kids were at their grandparents for the night, so Joe and I decided that it would be fun to go skinny dipping in the hot tub in our backyard. While the houses in our neighborhood are fairly close together, the fences are tall enough to ensure that there was no risk that our neighbors could see in. We were hanging out in the water, not thinking anything of it, when all the sudden we heard voices coming from our next-door neighbor's house.

It was no problem because we were confident they couldn't see through the fence, so we continued on.

What we didn't account for was the fact that the neighbors were not out in their backyard. They were, in fact, up on their roof. And it wasn't just our next-door neighbors. They had invited two other neighbors over to see if their roof had suffered any hail damage during a recent storm. I looked at Joe in a panic, hoping they hadn't seen us and contemplating how long I could hold my breath hiding under the water, when suddenly our neighbor yells down to us, "Good news, guys! No hail damage. Bad news is, Joe, you need a tan."

Yes, I officially contemplated convincing Joe that putting our house up for sale that very night and packing up our things and children and being gone before morning was the only option. Joe said that may be overreacting just a tiny bit. Thankfully we can all laugh about it now, but it took me a few years to get there.

The first time I saw Joe we were in college, and he almost fell off a cliff. I was out for a run along the coastline in San Diego when I noticed a hot, buff guy running toward me along the path. I had seen him around campus before, but my initial thought that day was that he was probably arrogant because of all the hotness and buffness. But then, just before he reached me, he tripped and nearly fell down the forty-foot cliff the path ran along. He hopped up and kept running without saying a word to me. He likes to joke that he fell for me the minute he saw me.

A few weeks later, he tracked down my phone number

through a mutual friend I had a class with in college and called me out of the blue using a cheesy pickup line to ask me out. It's a miracle that we have been married for nearly nineteen years, because it was touch and go at the beginning. Now that we are nearing the almost twenty-year mark of wearing each other's rings, young couples have started asking us for marriage advice. The problem is, I am of the opinion that it takes a good forty years of commitment to have any marriage street cred. We only have a few pieces of advice I feel confident passing along, but I will happily share them with you . . . as long as you promise to check back in another twenty years to get the really good stuff. In the meantime, here are some of the bits of wisdom about marriage that we've garnered over the years:

- Before the wedding, agree together as to what a reasonable number of pillows to decorate your bed is, because it is going to come up.
- Before you get married, listen carefully to the other person chewing. If you can stand that noise for the rest of your life, go ahead with the wedding.
- If one person has volunteered to cook something, *do not* critique their technique. Just turn away while they are cooking, then politely thank them for a delightfully prepared meal that you did not have to make yourself. The same goes for driving, changing dirty diapers, helping kids with their homework, and cleaning up throw-up.

- You can read all sorts of marriage books about how to be married, but not one book will tell you how to be married to *your person*. That is learned over time, so don't let anyone make you feel guilty if your marriage doesn't look like someone else's.[1]
- Healthy people ask for what they want. Don't be afraid to make a request.
- This one is big: recognize early on that you cannot make another person happy. You can make them smile, you can make them laugh, you can make them feel good, but whether a person is happy is out of your control. It is up to them.
- As for the important things you can bring to a marriage, kindness comes first, followed closely by a sense of humor.
- And lastly, our very best piece of advice is be like Bertha.

Bertha was married to a man who had big ideas but no business sense. He was an inventor who had a vision that could change the future, but the only problem was that no one else could see it. As financial stress grew, so did his self-doubt and depression. That's why Bertha decided to take her two sons on a road trip to see her mom.

She woke their kids, Richard and Ugen, before dawn and gathered supplies for the journey. She left a note for her hubby, telling him not to worry. Then she and her sons hit the road.

Hitting the road in those days was difficult, which

made the ride to Bertha's mom's place all the more exciting. The boys did a lot of pushing, as the car lacked traction on slick, grassy hills. Bertha made sure to steer them clear of ruts from horse-drawn carriages. Before long they ran out of fuel; there were no gas stations nearby, so she hiked to a pharmacy and bought some ligroin, a petroleum-based stain remover that might keep the car going. It did.

Not far from Bertha's mom's house the car stopped again; this time a clogged fuel line was the culprit. Bertha used one of her hairpins to fix the clog. A few minutes later, the car's electric ignition cable wore through, stopping them in their tracks. She removed her garter and used it to insulate the wire.

Fifteen hours after leaving their house, Bertha and her sons arrived at their destination. Richard and Ugen were thrilled to see their grandma, and after supper Bertha explained the crisis that confronted her family and her plan to solve it.

Bertha's mother was skeptical of her daughter's plan and begged her to be cautious. Her concern was justified, because on the way home, the car's brakes failed. Bertha cleverly found a local shoemaker, bought some leather strips, and had them nailed onto the wooden brake blocks. Problem solved.

When Bertha and her sons finally arrived back at the family home, her husband was waiting for her, but he wasn't alone. Word had spread far and wide of her journey, which is exactly why she decided to take it in the first place. Bertha had taken her sons on a 120-mile expedition at a time when the longest recorded road trip was approximately forty feet.

Word spread like wildfire, and within weeks newspapers all over the country were talking about Bertha's husband's invention. That was the summer of 1888. The automobile was the brainchild of a man named Carl Benz, who Bertha believed in with absolute certainty. Thanks to her, Mercedes Benz is still thriving today.[2]

Bertha was a daring woman who believed *for* her husband. She went on a daring adventure to prove it, and it changed everything for their family. Be like Bertha, because the greatest thing you can do for your spouse is to believe in them. Sometimes all it takes is one good adventure to spark a revolution of hope.

A ROMP IN THE OCEAN

It was April in San Diego and the middle of a season of discontent in our marriage. We had three kids under eight, Joe had an hour commute each way to work, and I was taking care of kids full-time while working part-time. The weight of a few tough years had caught up with us. Tension was high because we were both hurt and lonely (even though we wouldn't have said that at that time). Joe looked at me one night and said he didn't want to go on living like this anymore. It was the first and only time in our marriage that I felt scared it might not be forever.

I went to bed that night, and after tossing and turning for hours, I made a plan. I decided that while we were going to have to work hard to figure out a lot of things, the first thing that might help get us out of our funk was to do something a little crazy. Our ten-year anniversary was coming up in a month, which seemed like the perfect opportunity to infuse some levity into our lives. I called my photographer-friend, Michelle, hired a babysitter, and told Joe to meet us at the beach at 4:00 p.m. on Wednesday night.

This is where the fun starts. I pulled out my wedding dress and did my makeup, then headed with Michelle to meet Joe at the beach. Once I let him in on my plan, he was all in. That is the kind of guy he is, always ready for an unexpected adventure. I had brought some fun wedding-ish clothes for him to wear, and for the next two hours we ran along the beach, jumped in the waves, and sat in the sand, all in our formal wedding attire. It was exactly what we needed. Michelle took photos of the whole thing so we would have a reminder that when things got difficult in another ten years, we would not forget to make fun a priority.

Marriage, although a sacred endeavor, doesn't have to be so stuffy and serious. Sometimes what is needed is an unexpected romp in the ocean to remind you why you keep saying "I do."[3]

SNOW DAYS AND TIME-OUTS

I grew up in upstate New York, and one of the highlights of my childhood winters was snow days. I learned early on that a good snow day is made up of a few essential components. It starts out with a free pass on everything that is due at school that day. Then we go outside to play, followed by some type of delicious comfort food. It wraps up with a cozy huddle under warm blankets, watching feel-good television.

Occasionally, when things get too serious or heavy and it becomes essential to call a time-out from the normal pace of life, Joe and I now call for a self-imposed "snow day" for our marriage. It usually happens twice a year and has nothing to do with weather; instead, it is based entirely on the state of our emotional well-being. Here is how it plays out.

Joe or I declare it is time for a "snow day," which sets the plans into motion. We cancel our meetings for the next day, send our kids to school, and then he and I spend the day together. We take a hike with our dogs, go for a bike ride, or do something fun in the fresh air. Then we grab brunch or have the comfort food one of us is craving. After that we head home and take naps or watch a movie while drinking a warm beverage until our kids come home. That's when we pretend we've had a busy day at work.

Another tool that helps us reconnect is a good old-fashioned time-out. Time-outs are the result of having three children in a small house. Sometimes you need to talk about things without little ears hearing you, or perhaps you just need a good laugh when the day doesn't go as planned. This is how a little game called Meet Me came to be. Joe or I will randomly whisper "meet me" to the other person, making sure that no children are close enough to hear. Then we name a random rendezvous point where you are to meet that person in five minutes. Previous Meet Me spots have included the second branch of the tree in our front yard, the back seat of our car, and the roof. Mostly this is just a silly time out from the craziness of the day, but it is also a fun secret that no one else knows about, which adds some thrill to the routine of parenting.

BRINGING SEXY BACK

I mentioned earlier that we try to keep the fire alive in our marriage, and I am all about sending a suggestive text every once in a while. My only fear is that one of my children might intercept it, and then they'll have to invest in years of therapy as an adult to work through the resulting trauma. I had an experience that made me skittish about this whole topic recently when I was at the grocery store with one of my kids and noticed that I was getting a call while we were checking out. It was Joe calling; not wanting to be rude to the cashier, I handed my phone to my daughter and asked her to answer. She did, but there was silence on the other end. That's when in front of everyone in line, the person scanning our groceries, and the teenager bagging them up she said, "Mom, I think Dad just booty-called you." *Ummmm*, and then instantly it hit me.

"Do you mean, Dad just butt dialed me?" Thank goodness she had no clue what she had actually said.

In addition to sexy texts, here are a few other ideas for keeping things interesting in the romance department:

- Instead of going straight for home base, set a timer for fifteen minutes and agree that the only thing you can do during that time is kiss. Kissing is bonding and super hot, but often we forget how awesome it can be.
- Out in public, randomly pull your guy into a doorway or alley and give him a passionate kiss just to surprise him. There is something about him not expecting it that makes it that much more exciting.

GO ON MORE DATES

Lastly, I can't write about marriage without throwing in fun date-night ideas. This is one of the most prosaic ways to have more fun when you're married, but sometimes you have to stick with the tried-and-true ideas that work. Being alone with your partner can create more moments that make you remember why you chose each other in the first place, loud chewing and all.

Here are three ideas that will make you want to go on more dates.

Fancy Thrift-Store Dinner. Our friends Emma and Jake decided that their date routine had gotten stale. Instead of the normal dinner and a movie, they went to a thrift store and each got $15 to pick out an outfit for the other person. Hilarity ensued when they each changed into their outfit and headed out to a fancy dinner, where they made a scene . . . and also a memory they won't soon forget.

First Date. No, this isn't about recreating your first date. This is about pretending it is your first date. Get ready separately. Then meet up somewhere unexpected and pretend you don't know each other. Ask all the first-date questions, like "What do you do?" and "Where did you grow up?" Then, at the end of the night, invite your spouse back to your place for "extracurricular activities." Fingers crossed.

Personality Quizzes. Instead of binge-watching Netflix together, try getting to know each other better by taking free online personality tests. All it takes is some googling. My favorites are the Enneagram, the Myers-Briggs Type Indicator, StrengthsFinder, and the 5 Love Languages.

Remember . . . be kind to yourself. When marriage is not all rose petals and negligees, it can be hard to have fun. When your relationship is painful or unbearably difficult, seek the resources you need to survive and thrive. You deserve it.

CHAPTER 6

HAVE MORE FUN WHEN THINGS DON'T GO AS PLANNED

What it all comes down to is that everything's
gonna to be fine, fine, fine.

ALANIS MORISSETTE

I t all started when my friend drank her contacts one morning. She had been traveling all night, thanks to a delayed flight, and when she finally made it to the hotel, it was 4:00 a.m. She had only a few hours to sleep until her work meeting in the morning. She slept through her alarm and was startled awake by sunlight streaming through the windows . . . an hour after her meeting was supposed to start. She was so disoriented that she took a quick drink of water from the glass on the nightstand, only to remember a second too late that it was, in fact, saline with a contact chaser.

After some panicked googling, she decided it would be wise to swing by urgent care to make sure the contacts and saline weren't going to be a problem. As she sat in the Uber, heading to the nearest doctor while her contacts were digesting in her stomach, her laughter turned to self-loathing. She berated herself, questioning, *Why do I continually get myself into these dumb situations?* Her guilt (about being late to her meeting) and embarrassment (about drinking her contacts) brought her to tears. Luckily, the kind Uber driver noticed her crying in the rearview mirror and gently asked if everything was OK. As she told him the story, he listened sympathetically, then said, "Sounds like you've had a pretty exciting morning. Bad day, but not a bad life. Maybe you need to be more comfortable with the surprises of being human." A sage prophet sitting behind the wheel of a Camry. Surprisingly, the doctor she saw had similar feedback. He reassured her that more people drink their contacts than you would have guessed, and that all would be well.

Bad day, not a bad life.

THE SCIENCE OF HAPPINESS

Sometimes it is small things that don't go as planned, like drinking our contacts and being late to a meeting. Other times, the circumstances surrounding us are so big it makes us feel like life as we know it is imploding right before our eyes. We are tempted to believe that we will never have fun or be happy again. I was there not long ago. My dad died, my husband and I lost a business, and our financial lives disintegrated over the course of a few years. During that time, I watched Dan Gilbert's TED talk, "The Surprising Science of Happiness."[1] In it, he shares scientific research that is so counterintuitive, it shook the bad-life projections I had been calculating right out of my head.

Gilbert and his research team found that our happiness is not dependent on what happens to us. In fact, they discovered that one year after their life-altering experience, both lottery winners and paraplegics reported the same levels of happiness. Let that sink in for a minute. A year after winning the lottery you would be as happy as a newly adapting paraplegic. Or a year after becoming a paraplegic, you would be as happy as someone who won the lottery.

Gilbert goes on to say that

the research that my laboratory has been doing, that economists and psychologists around the country have been doing, has revealed something really quite startling to us. . . . From field studies to laboratory studies, we see that winning or losing an election, gaining or losing a romantic partner, getting or not getting a promotion, passing or not passing a college test, on and on, have far less impact, less intensity, and much less duration than people expect them to have.

This almost floors me—a recent study showing how major life traumas affect people suggests that if it happened over three months ago, with only a few exceptions, it has no impact whatsoever on your happiness.[2]

I have been known to put a lot of emphasis on the circumstances of my day, assuming that what does or doesn't happen will determine how happy I feel. But what I am learning is that our baseline happiness can be increased not by having cool things happen to us but by merely choosing to find the fun and joy in the midst of the hard stuff, because the opportunity for fun is always there.

My dad died unexpectedly when I was twenty. I was in shock, but there was so much laughter, hugging, and joke telling at my dad's funeral, right alongside the tears and grief, that I almost couldn't distinguish where one started and the other ended, which, by the way, is exactly how my dad would have wanted it. People we didn't know stocked our fridge for weeks, friends helped us move (the ultimate act of sacrifice), my mom even rented jet skis for our whole family a month after the funeral as an act of defiance. It was her declaration that grief and sorrow didn't have the final word, and if Dad were there he would have been the first one out on the water. Heartbreak and fun mingled together, because life is typically both.

When Joe and I were broke and eating canned chili for dinner, we would dine by candlelight and toast to being happy even though we were stressed. We knew that, in time, we would remember those moments with fondness and tenderness for having made it through. More than ten years later, we totally do.

LOVE THE SHIRT, HATE THE PANTS

Voltaire has been credited as saying, "The most important decision you make each day is the decision to be in a good mood." I think that's good, but he could do better. Just because you are a philosophical savant, whose work has been regarded for nearly four hundred years as a catalyst to the Enlightenment, doesn't mean you don't need help occasionally. Choosing to be in a good mood is powerful; choosing fun when things don't go as planned is life-changing.

One of the most challenging times to choose fun is when we are embarrassed. This is a daily opportunity in my life and one that spills over onto the people I love most. Without a doubt, one of the things my kids will remember most about their childhood is the frequency with which I embarrass them. Recently all three of my children grew out of every item of clothing they own at the same time, which meant that I got to take all three children shopping at the same time. Did I mention that I loathe shopping? This is why, when I saw something cute for me while I was supposed to be shopping for my kids, I decided to try it on, so that I wouldn't have to make a separate trip to the God-forsaken no-man's-land known as the mall.

With the item in hand, I gathered my kids, convinced them it would only take a minute, and headed to the dressing rooms. Now, the dressing rooms in this particular store were so small that I could barely squeeze my purse in with me, let alone my three children, so I had them line up against the wall right outside and employed the technique where you talk with them the whole time so you know they are OK. I changed into this new item of clothing as fast as I could, opened the door, and started scanning my kids' faces to get a thumbs-up or -down on whether it was a keeper. As I did, a darling teenage girl who worked at the store made a beeline over to me, put her finger to her lips for a moment, and then pointed to each item I was wearing as she said, "Love the shirt, hate the pants."

"Cool, cool, cool. Thank you for the feedback," I said, faking a nonchalant attitude.

The problem was, the pants she hated were *my* pants. As in, the pants I wore into the store.

At that moment I felt like I was right back to last week—you thought I was going to say high school, right? Nope, last week—when I was practicing an important speech in the bathroom mirror at work with as much animation and confidence as I could assemble. I wanted to see how it would come across on stage. Halfway through, a guest who was visiting our office walked in on me because I forgot to lock the door. I told you this happens frequently.

Meanwhile, back in the store, my kids were humiliated that their mom was wearing lame pants, but they were equally empathetic toward my embarrassing plight. As soon as the teenage fashionista walked away, my middle daughter offered, "Mom, this feels like something that would happen on *The Goldbergs* [our favorite TV show]." This immediately sparked my memory. Just a few weeks earlier, my friend Melanie and I were talking about how to reframe our thinking when things don't go as planned. She said she regularly asks herself, *If this situation was happening to my favorite sitcom character, would I laugh at it?*

The answer in this situation was yes, I would find it hilarious. Same with swallowing contacts. Life is like a sitcom, so we might as well laugh at it. The problem is that my natural instinct is to feel other feelings bigger. I really love to be in control. I like to know I have thought through all possible scenarios and have planned for every possible variation of events. And I especially like when people think I am cool. I have to process through these emotions like anger, embarrassment, and shame before I get to laughter. Finding a way to laugh when someone else gets embarrassed? Easy. Finding genuine laughter when I am the main character in the story? Much harder.

I walked into the dressing room, put my top back on, walked out, and sat on the floor outside of the dressing room with my kids. I started laughing so hard I couldn't breathe. They joined me, and we laughed so extravagantly we had to leave the store because we were making a scene. None of us can try on anything in a store now without one of us offering, "Love the shirt, hate the pants."

FUN DISSIPATES EMBARRASSMENT

I know two women who became best friends after they showed up at a wedding in the same dress. At first, they were both so embarrassed they tried to stay on different sides of the room in hopes that no one would notice. But then one of them recognized the shared absurdity of the situation. She walked over and convinced the other to join her for a funny picture to memorialize their fashion *faux pas*, and they have been best friends ever since. That was twenty-two years ago.

One of my reoccurring mom-stress dreams revolves around the high-stakes game of hosting a kid birthday party. The catalyst for this dream was a five-year-old's party I attended with my oldest daughter. In the middle of the party, it was time to begin the much-beloved hitting of the piñata. The only problem was that when those kids busted through the colorful unicorn, there was no candy flying. The mom (aka, the party hostess) had assumed that the piñata came prefilled. The result was a gaggle of five-year-olds, crying over unspilt candy. The moms at the party rallied, as moms do, and pulled candy from the bottom of our purses and cars. One mom who lived next door ran to her house and grabbed her personal stash of chocolate. We taped up that piñata, filled it with the community candy, and happiness was restored.

Let me be clear, not one of the moms there felt one ounce of remorse that those kids were crying over candy.

We all agreed that none of those precious children needed even one Skittle. The reason we did it was because the party-hosting mom needed a win.

Later that year, when the hostess's birthday came around, we threw another party. The theme was piñatas. We had a piñata filled with candy, one filled with small trinkets and toys, and the biggest one was filled to the brim with all her favorite things. It was the best party I have ever been to, and afterward she said that she finally was able to get over her embarrassment over the first piñata disaster. Fun has a way of dissipating embarrassment.

We can turn our embarrassment into friendship and lame pants into an unforgettable moment. The power is in our response.

HOW ARE YOU TRAINING YOUR MIND?

The idea that our lives should be a certain way is one thing that can suck the fun out of our experience with unprecedented ease. A few key components of our vision board don't pan out, or we aren't where we thought we would be at this stage of life, and we get laser focused on what is missing. Not fun. Perhaps it is a relationship that ended or a job we hate. Maybe we don't feel like we are doing anything meaningful, or our savings account has the same balance as our kid's lunch account at school.

When we only focus on what is lacking, we fail to notice the things that are good in our lives. While it sounds like feel-good positive psychology, the truth is that what we focus on expands. It becomes larger, because we are actively looking for it.

I had two professors in college who were good friends. One was a Jesuit priest with a black belt in jiujitsu. The other taught Hebrew along with classes on peaceful reconciliation, and he was a fun-loving running aficionado who always talked about the beauty of San Diego. One day they shared a story about going to the mall together to watch a movie on a Friday night. After the movie, the martial-artist priest kept making comments about how many shady people there were at the mall. He sensed that everyone seemed on edge, forcing him to be on guard so he would be ready to use his skills in case anything dangerous went down. On the other hand, the Hebrew teacher noted how beautiful the evening was and how everyone seemed so happy to be outside after a long week of rain. He thought it was moving to see people from all walks of life congregate to share a meal or people watch. These two men walked the same path, saw the same movie, and interacted with the same people, yet they had completely different experiences. They each saw what they had trained their minds to notice.

We see the world based on what we train our minds to believe. If the narrative you have on repeat in your head is "I am unlucky in love," then you probably will be. Or if you believe you'll never have enough money, you most likely won't. Our brains are powerful and want to prove us right. That is why changing the way our minds interpret our circumstances is essential to adapting when things don't go as planned. To do this, when you encounter an unforeseen event, ask yourself, *What if my problem isn't a problem?*

I recently met a guy who had been diagnosed with a severe form of mono in the middle of his senior year of high school, ten years earlier. He had been a football player, and he missed his entire senior season. He didn't get to go to prom or do any of the things he'd been anticipating; those activities took a back seat to sleep and getting well. For the first few weeks after his diagnosis, he was depressed and devastated, but then he decided that he wasn't going to feel like a victim. Instead he decided to see mono and the resting it required as a gift that he could use for good. He set a goal to write a letter to every single member of his senior class, telling them each three things he appreciated about them. He shared with me that he had just attended his ten-year reunion a few months before, and at the reunion no one talked about whether they won the homecoming football game or who they took to prom. But you know what everyone remembered about their senior year? The letters he wrote them. Sounds pretty fun to have that kind of impact.

What do we do when we are in the in-between space of disappointment? Just wait it out until we're on to something better? The fun response is to do what we can, with what we have, where we are right now. Stop waiting for what you think you need, and start working with what you've got.

Because maybe your problem isn't a problem; maybe it's an opportunity for fun.

CHAPTER 7

HAVE MORE FUN WITH WORK

In every job that must be done, there is an element of fun.

MARY POPPINS

The thing about life is one day you are cool and fun, and then the next day you have a favorite grocery store and a breast pump in your desk drawer at work. It all happens very fast. I have a tendency to believe that whatever is true in my life right now is how it will always be, but then before I know it and without a lot of intention, another life emerges that I couldn't have imagined even a few years before.

I started working when I was seventeen at Perkins in upstate New York, serving pancakes to drunk people who were heading home from the bar at 2:00 a.m. In the years between waitressing and now CEO, I have done it all. Worked full time, stayed at home with my kids, worked part time while raising kids, been the primary breadwinner, not been the primary breadwinner. In every different season, one thing I have learned is that all work is important, but no work, regardless of how virtuous it is, is worth losing life's spontaneity and joy.

Which is why I have deemed Theodore Roosevelt the patron saint of fun at work, to remind us all of what is possible. Reflecting on his time as President of the United States, he wrote, "I have had the best time of any man of my age in all the world. . . . I have enjoyed myself in the White House, more than I have ever known any other President to enjoy himself."[1]

Theodore Roosevelt lived out his passions, did memorable work, and prioritized his family, all of which is evidenced by some unusual facts you might not know about him.

He took responsibility for his happiness. As a freshman in college he wrote his mother a letter, and in it he wrote, "It seems perfectly wonderful, in looking back over my eighteen years of existence to see how I have literally never spent an unhappy day, unless by my own fault." Years after that, he famously said, "The joy of living is his who has the heart to demand it."[2]

He made family and fun a priority. In the spring of 1903 Roosevelt's nine-year-old son Archie, who was the fifth of his six children, was recovering from the measles. Earlier that year, Archie had received a Shetland pony from the Secretary of the Interior, Ethan Allen Hitchcock, as a gift. Archie named him Algonquin. Measuring thirty-three inches in height at the withers and weighing in at 350 pounds, Algonquin was described by the *Washington Post* as "iron gray with spots and compactly built with a round barrel, small ears, clean pony face, and stocky limbs." The reporter went on to say that "Algonquin is a very good-natured, though spirited little beast."[3] One day, having been confined to his bed for weeks recovering from measles, Archie asked his mother if he could visit Algonquin. After deciding Archie wasn't strong enough to venture into the stable, a different plan was hatched. They decided to bring the pony to the boy by walking Algonquin into the White House, squeezing him into the elevator and taking him to Archie's bedroom that was on the second floor. Archie shouted with joy, and Algonquin had an adventure that no other horse has ever had, because family and fun were prioritized in the White House during Roosevelt's terms. Work and fun happened right alongside one another. Next time things feel a little off at your office, might I suggest a few pony rides around the parking lot as a quick pick-me-up? Not joking. Or maybe have everyone bring their dogs to work and have a puppy party—because snuggling furry friends can diffuse even the most serious budget conversations.

He was persistent. In 1912 Roosevelt delivered a rousing campaign speech, after having been shot a few moments earlier. Teddy was a popular president throughout his two terms in office, which lasted from 1901 to

1909. But not everyone loved him. At one campaign stop in Milwaukee, a bar owner named John Schrank approached Teddy as he walked to the podium, drew a pistol, and shot the former president in the chest. It would have been a fatal wound, were it not for Teddy's crumpled, handwritten speech tucked in the breast pocket of his shirt; the document thwarted the bullet, and Teddy only suffered a flesh wound. With the bullet fragments still lodged in his torso, Teddy took to the stage and delivered a rousing speech that lasted for nearly an hour; after he stepped down from the stage woozy from blood loss, he was rushed to a nearby hospital. After being treated for the wound, Roosevelt got back to it.[4] He continued on the campaign trail because nothing would stop Roosevelt from pursuing the work he felt called to do. I had a urinary tract infection a few months ago that was really terrible, and I showed up at work before the antibiotics kicked in, so pretty much samesies.

He went skinny dipping in the Potomac. This is by far one of my favorite facts about Teddy. During his presidency, the notorious outdoorsman regularly escaped the confines of the White House by sailing his presidential yacht on the Potomac for his lunch break. If he wasn't sailing, he could be found leading a hike in Rock Creek Park, and regularly after strenuous walks along the Potomac the president would leave his clothes on the shore and take a dip in the river to cool off, #spiritanimal. You can see now why I chose him as all-time patron saint of fun at work, especially for the way he crushed his lunch break.

Lastly, he made first moves. There is a well-known theory in chess called the first-move advantage that suggests the player who goes first is statistically positioned for the best outcome. Theodore Roosevelt lived this theory. He was the first president to refer to the presidential mansion as the White House, the first president to host a black man at a White House dinner, and the first to appoint a Jewish person as a cabinet member. He was also the first president to travel outside the United States while in office, and the first American to win a Nobel Peace Prize.[5] Don't forget the first to bring a pony into the White House for an elevator ride because it was going to make his kid's day.

Theodore Roosevelt lived his life with gusto and didn't worry too much about what anyone else thought about it. He was determined that his work would be remarkable, his family would thrive, and all the while he would have the most fun that anyone has ever had. How did he accomplish it? He did it by doing things that no one else did and making first moves.

Here are five first moves to make to have more fun and kick butt at work.

MOVE ONE: LEAVE THEM ASKING, "WHO THE HECK DOES SHE THINK SHE IS?"

I have a friend who is so disarming and confident that when people interact with her for the first time, they leave the conversation asking, "Who the heck does she think she is?" They are simultaneously confused and smitten at the same time. Have you ever met someone like this? They are the kind of people who end up backstage at a concert because they act like they should be there and no one questions them. They land meetings with people they admire because they are gutsy and believe anything is possible. All you have to do is ask.

I have always admired people like this because I've spent most of my years overanalyzing everything I said and did. If I said something weird to you once when I was twenty, rest assured I spent every night for the next ten years thinking about it. All of that changed, however, when I decided that "who the heck does she think she is" looked a lot more fun than "is Jen's grandma, who I don't know except from soccer practice pick-up and drop-off, offended that I said her new lip filler looks natural?" This type of ridiculousness should not take up one moment of brain space, am I right?

What I have discovered since I decided not to worry about Jen's grandma's feelings about her lip filler anymore is that living a "who the heck does she think she is" kind of life can be learned. You don't have to be naturally confident or charismatic. It starts with small baby steps. Before you know it, you will be backstage on a movie set, swapping makeup tips with Candace Cameron Bure, or sharing heartfelt stories with Ben Higgins from *The Bachelor* while sitting on the blue couch in your office. True story.

A simple way to get started is to commit to making one audacious ask a week. Maybe it is asking for a discount at the grocery store, or sending a note to your favorite author asking to have coffee, or submitting a résumé for your dream job even though you don't have the required experience. You'll know that you are on the right track when it makes your palms sweat.

When you don't ask, you lose by default and you'll never know the opportunities that were missed. What is the worst that could happen? They say no. What is the best that could happen? You get what you ask for. This is my favorite kind of first move because you really can't lose. Put yourself out there, and I am confident you will be blown away by what happens.

MOVE TWO: PUT WORK INTO THE WORLD THAT IS UNEXPECTEDLY EXTRAORDINARY

As kids, we use our imagination to dream up what is possible. As adults, we use our imagination to dream up all the terrible things that might go wrong. We squander our imagination on worry instead of using it to create something that no one else has ever thought of. A critical first move to remedy this is to put work into the world that challenges what everyone expects.

There is a hotel in LA that is painted canary yellow, has a pool roughly the size of an elementary school four-square grid, and is a converted two-story apartment building built in the 1950s. And did I mention that it doesn't have an elevator? Also, it is one of the highest rated hotels in LA. Out of 3,264 reviews (as of 3 August 2018) on TripAdvisor, nearly 84% of people rated it as either excellent or very good. Pretty impressive for a little hotel that is competing with big chains like the Four Seasons and the Marriot.

Let me introduce you to the Magic Castle Hotel and their underwhelming accommodations but extraordinary ability to make a hotel stay something you will remember for the rest of your life.

The Magic Castle Hotel's trick in capturing the heart and positive reviews of the people who stay there is found in a term coined by Chip and Dan Heath in their book *The Power of Moments*; Magic Castle has learned how to be "occasionally remarkable."[6] There is a cherry red phone mounted to a wall near the pool. Pick it up, and someone answers, "Hello, popsicle hotline." You then place your order, and minutes later a staffer wearing white gloves delivers your popsicles with your flavors of choice on a silver tray, at no cost.

You can drop off unlimited loads of laundry for free, and your clothes will be returned later in the day, wrapped in twine with a sprig of lavender. There is a snack menu filled with all the treats both kids and adults love, which can also be enjoyed at no additional cost. If you want something special for breakfast, just let them know, and they will make sure it is waiting for you when you come down in the morning, and of course it is all complimentary. Not to mention that three times a week, magicians perform tricks at breakfast just because it is fun.

There are countless families who after a week of staying in LA, visiting Disney and Universal Studios and the Pacific Ocean, go home and ask their kids what their favorite part of the trip was, only to hear their kids recounting how the popsicle hotline was the highlight of the week. Why is this? Because sometimes a little extra attention to unusual details can make all the difference in creating something remarkable.

Every single detail doesn't have to be perfect, because monotony doesn't register in our minds. Our minds are looking for peak experiences where something significant stands out and stays with us. This is interesting to think about. Instead of trying to do everything moderately well, what matters is focusing on a few important things and doing them spectacularly and with gusto. The Magic Castle Hotel knows that work and fun can happen at the same time, and so they don't worry too much about the things that aren't perfect; they care about doing some unexpected things that no one else is doing to stand out.

MOVE THREE: ELEVATE INSTEAD OF COMMISERATE

I am going to shoot straight with this one. Your happiness at work is your responsibility; you are in control of it.

One of the most potent ways I believe we own our joy at work is to reject the norm that says that we need to join another person's pity party. Instead of commiserating, our first move can be instead to elevate the conversation. Rather than, "You poor thing, I am in the same boat," we say, "Got it, hear you, and guess what? Yes, you can do it. I am standing with you. We are going to make it happen together."

When we actively change the energy of a conversation from negative to empowered, we are better positioned to deal with anything the day can throw at us. Not to mention that we are way more inspiring to be around.

MOVE FOUR: PLAY THE LONG GAME

One thing I get asked about a lot is my work. I lead an organization that has huge influence around the world, which means I have opportunities to travel, meet cool people, write books, and do awesome stuff. It also means that I regularly have people ask how I landed said job, or how they can have the job when I leave, which is understandable because it is a freaking awesome gig.

But one thing I rarely talk about are the years and years of writing things that no one read, taking jobs that were far from what I wanted to be doing, and getting up to work at 4:00 a.m. so I could be present when my kids woke up. What I have learned over the years about work and pursuing passions and chasing success is that life is about the long game. So often we want immediate gratification for the hard work we are putting in. What experience has shown me, however, is that getting "there," whatever "there" is for each of us, usually means doing the next small thing with excellence, not thinking anything is beneath us, and doing our work with heart and passion, even if we feel like no one is paying attention.

Not long ago, Rachel Hollis, founder of the Hollis Company, posted this caption about work and playing the long game in one of her Instagram posts. She wrote:

> Someone asked me on a podcast recently how it felt to be an "overnight success." I had to stop myself from giggling. I've been building this company and this platform for 14 years. I'm an "overnight success" after a decade and a half of working on it. Don't think that any of this came easy or quickly or without an incredible amount of hard work. You want big dreams? You're gonna have to put in big hours. You want a life that few people can claim? You're gonna have to do the work that few people will. Have patience, learn from the journey, put your head down, and get back to work.[7]

I would add, get back to work and enjoy yourself more than you have ever known any other person to enjoy themselves doing it. Don't worry too much about whether it is your dream job or if it will help you get ahead; don't get too tripped up by road bumps or disappointment that it isn't happening as fast as you would like. Even though you aren't where you want to be doesn't mean that you can't enjoy where you are. Just keep showing up, doing your work and being adamant about adding a little fun as you go. If you are daring, try taking a dip in the Potomac on your lunch break.

I can't continue without giving a quick shout-out to you moms who are reading this and don't feel like you are doing anything important with your life. You have always wanted to write a book or run a company or go back to school, but this season of your life requires something different. Let me say this to you: nothing is more important than loving your people. Writing a book? You are writing the lives of the small humans you are caring for into existence. Running a company? You are running the equivalent of five companies with the number of details you manage every day. Be present in the season you are in and never underestimate the importance of loving your people well, because that is the only legacy, the only byline, the only profit statement that lasts.

MOVE FIVE: MAKE MISCHIEF

This is a simple one. Want to thrive at work? Make mischief with your coworkers.

My love language is pranks. For my birthday a few years ago, my coworkers covered everything in my office in wrapping paper. Individual paper clips were wrapped, each marker on my whiteboard, my entire desk, each folder, every pen, pictures on the wall, each book, plants, the trash can, everything. It took them hours and hours, and I am still smiling about it. It was one of the best gifts I have ever received.

My friend Elizabeth used to work at a company where they had a tradition each year where all the employees would bring desserts to a Thanksgiving celebration. They had a very loud and energetic team, whose method of showing endearment was giving one another a hard time. One year, a coworker named Sara bought a cake from a local bakery as her contribution to the feast. The cake turned out to be a colossal mistake, primarily because it tasted like fruity meat. At first, everyone at the celebration tried to be gracious and appreciative that she went out of her way to contribute to the meal, but when Sara took a bite, she immediately used some very colorful language while picking it up and marching it straight out to the trash can. When she walked back into the office, she reprimanded everyone for being nice but not honest. "Don't you ever pretend to like something I bring, I mean it," she chastised them. At the next office Thanksgiving celebration and every Thanksgiving since, Sara brings the worst store-bought cake she can find, and the rest of the staff give out a fake Oscar (a Barbie doll painted gold) to whoever does the best job pretending they like what she brings. She thinks it is hilarious, and it makes her grateful every year that she works with such fun-loving people.

I don't know if there is science to back this claim up, but I have seen how more fun with colleagues means more success at work. Go ahead and make the first move.

THE OG LADY BOSS

There are so many expectations of what a woman should be and shouldn't be. What a good mom should do and shouldn't do, especially regarding work. If you add God into the equation, there is potential for the conversation to get even more complicated. That is why for a long time, I rebelled against the idea of what a lot of people of faith refer to as a "Proverbs 31" woman. Here is the issue. I have a tendency to be a little salty and a lot unconventional, and the way most Christian women talk about being a Proverbs 31 woman sounded to my ears like it was a mixture of *The Handmaid's Tale*, a Stepford wife, and the annoying mom at school whose kids have never eaten candy. Stay with me.

Then I reread Proverbs 31 last year, and something new jumped out at me. Here's an excerpt:

> *A wife of noble character who can find?*
> *She is worth far more than rubies.*
> *Her husband has full confidence in her*
> *and lacks nothing of value.*
> *She brings him good, not harm,*

all the days of her life.
She selects wool and flax
and works with eager hands.
She is like the merchant ships,
bringing her food from afar.
She gets up while it is still night;
she provides food for her family
and portions for her female servants.
She considers a field and buys it;
out of her earnings, she plants a vineyard.
She sets about her work vigorously;
her arms are strong for her tasks.
She sees that her trading is profitable,
and her lamp does not go out at night.

She makes linen garments and sells them,
and supplies the merchants with sashes.
She is clothed with strength and dignity;
she can laugh at the days to come.
(Proverbs 31:10–18, 24–25)

Let me break it down.

She gets up, she provides for her family and the people who work with her, she does her research, she kills it at trading, she makes cool stuff (who doesn't love a good sash?), she is strong, dignified, and—*she laughs.*

She is the OG Lady Boss! (OG stands for "original gangster" for those who don't know.)

She is our people. You and me and all the other women out there, showing up every day and doing the work God has given us. Whether we are leading from the boardroom or a kitchen table, or getting up when it's dark to take the bus to a job because right now it is the way God has given us to put food on the table, we are all Proverbs 31 in action. We are resourceful and persistent, but most importantly we always find a reason to laugh.

Now, go out there and be like Teddy and our OG lady boss and get after it.

SEVEN WAYS TO HAVE
MORE FUN AT WORK

1. Be like Janella at my office who rides her scooter through the halls because it is more fun than walking.
2. Play some pranks on coworkers. Googly eyes are a great way to start.
3. Display an awkward photo of you from your childhood, teens, or early twenties on your desk.
4. Leave Post-it notes with silly jokes or fun facts inside bathroom stalls.
5. Sneak anonymous, encouraging notes to your work nemesis.
6. Put fresh flowers on the desk of someone who needs them.
7. Have mandatory Popsicle breaks planned once a week.

CHAPTER 8

HAVE MORE FUN WITH SELF-IMPROVEMENT

Mad Hatter: "Have I gone mad?"
Alice: "I'm afraid so. You're entirely bonkers.
But I'll tell you a secret. All the best people are."
TIM BURTON'S *ALICE IN WONDERLAND*

My Amazon shopping cart is a pretty accurate glimpse into the state of my life on any given day. Right now, for example, it contains a weighted blanket I'm thinking about buying to help me sleep, because I have a little anxiety with a side of waking up at 3:00 a.m. There are three confetti cannons that I have big plans to use at bus pick-up next month to celebrate National Hairball Awareness Day (the last Friday in April, FYI). This is a real thing that my kids think is hilarious, so I am planning accordingly.

Because Jane Austen fan fiction is my current jam—I probably shouldn't admit that—there are two novels in my queue of must-reads. To top it off, there is a jade Yoni Egg, which Gwyneth Paltrow says will make my sex life better and help me not pee when I sneeze.

The reason I have all these things in my cart, and not on their way to my home, is because I like to give myself a cooling-off period before I make purchases, since my financial sensibilities swing wildly from "I need to save money" to "you only live once." Top that off with the fact that I am a sucker for any new self-improvement product, and you can see that this is a vital part of my Amazon shopping experience.

Isn't it thrilling to know that if you are too busy to run to the store for Scotch tape, you can order it online? Some mystery person will put it on a plane, it will be flown to your local distribution center, get loaded on a truck, and be driven ten miles (give or take) to your door . . . in a box that is three times too big and filled with nonbiodegradable plastic packing material to ensure that the two rolls of tape you could have purchased from the grocery store a mile away makes it to your doorstep safely. Truly, this is real progress.

Everything we need is a click away. We have the entire knowledge of humanity in a handheld device that we carry around with us everywhere we go. We have a constant stream of content on social media providing suggestions for "five ways to have better sex" or "everything you need to accomplish before turning forty," and yet everyone I talk to has never felt more discontent or more neurotic.

This conundrum started to make sense after I read an article in the *New Yorker* titled "Improving Ourselves to Death" by Alexandra Schwartz. In it, she talks about the implications of living in a consumerist society and our resulting tendency to never be satisfied with our purchases or ourselves:

> "In a consumerist society, we are not meant to buy one pair of jeans and then be satisfied," Cederström and Spicer write, and the same, they think, is true of self-improvement. We are being sold on the need to upgrade all parts of ourselves, all at once, including parts that we did not previously know needed upgrading. (This may explain Yoni eggs, stone vaginal inserts that purport to strengthen women's pelvic-floor muscles and take away "negative energy." Gwyneth Paltrow's website, Goop, offers them in both jade and rose quartz.) There is a great deal of money to be made by those who diagnose and treat our fears of inadequacy; Cederström and Spicer estimate that the self-improvement industry takes in ten billion dollars a year.[1]

A counselor friend told me that the most resisted advice she offers clients who are feeling inadequate, depressed, overwhelmed, or anxious is to give themselves a one-month break from any type of self-improvement, and instead to do something every day that feels fun. While it is the hardest advice for her clients to embrace, she says it turns out to be the single most effective treatment plan she offers.

Apparently, the way to have more fun with self-improvement is to stop and start. Here's what it looks like.

STOP FOCUSING ON SELF-IMPROVEMENT AND START HAVING MORE FUN

A friend of mine has been trying to lose fifteen pounds for as long as I've known her. She recently canceled her gym membership because she hates going to the gym. For her, the gym has always felt like punishment, and seeing all the tight twenty-year-old butts on the treadmills made her feel angry and a little desperate. For the last few years she's wanted to take tango lessons, but it felt frivolous to spend time and money on it, so she pushed it to the back of her mind. That is, until a month ago, when she took the money from her gym membership and invested it into three months of tango lessons. A week ago, I had a voicemail from her telling me that she has never had more fun and that she has lost five pounds without even trying. She is having the time of her life and has never felt more vibrant or alive.

STOP KEEPING SCORE AND START MAKING A BETTER LIST

I am really good at inventing ways to keep score of whether I am winning or losing, improving or failing. Annual goals are my jam, and checking items off my to-do list is as addictive as smoking crack—I'm guessing; I have never actually smoked crack. Our self-improvement culture promotes this kind of measuring. Count your steps, journal your dreams, tweak your diet, log your sleep rhythms, then analyze the data, recalibrate, and repeat the whole process the next day.[2] The whole thing is exhausting.

This is why, for one month, I have vowed to create a better list. Instead of listing all the items I already know need to get done or adding more self-improvement practices to my lengthy list of to-dos, I started to make a list of fun things I want to add to my life:

- Look up silly jokes to tell my kids at breakfast.
- Be the first person to cannonball into the pool this weekend.
- Pick my kids up from school early on a Friday and take them on a surprise road trip.
- Get up early and drink hot chocolate. Because it is delicious, and I want to savor it before the hustle and bustle of the morning.
- Bake some bread and deliver it to my neighbors.

It might seem trite or silly, but I call it prioritizing what I will remember when I am on my deathbed. I probably won't be super proud of the extra emails I returned, but I will undoubtedly remember the surprise food fight I started one night at dinner, and so will my kids.

The other thing I am choosing to remember about measuring success is that many of the mundane tasks of life will never be finished once and for all, and that is OK. My friend Leeana Tankersley explains this so beautifully in her book *Begin Again*:

> We love the idea of doing things once and for all, but this is not where meaning is found. We don't take communion once and for all. We don't love our spouse once and for all. We don't parent once and for all. We don't do the dishes or the laundry or the vacuuming once and for all. We don't read, endure the commute, or shave our legs once and for all. We return, in what turns out to be a sacred connection, to the mundane task, to the moment. And then we do it again. Over and over. Again. This is the raw material of our living. And none of it is to be overlooked. This is not insanity or hilarity or nuisance or idiocy. This is the task of humanity. To return. To reinvest. To breathe. To begin again. The focus is on the process, the participation, not the product. Ever.[3]

STOP CHECKING YOUR PHONE AND START TAKING THE SLOW LANE

Chronic distraction is our generation's drug of choice. Statistics say that, on average, Americans check their phone once every twelve minutes, or eighty times a day.[4] Crazy, right? If you want a stark reality check about your own phone usage, download an app like Moment (that tracks how many minutes you spend on your phone each day) or Checky (that tells you how often you unlock your phone).

For many of us, smartphones are the remote controls of our lives. They help us with our work, store our important data, and help us to have access to any information we need the moment we need it. The goal of technology has always been to make us more efficient and give us more free time, but I know very few people who will say this is the result. Instead we are all busier and less connected.

One way to push back against the consumerism and distraction of our phones is to take the slow lane. This is not a new idea. During the nineteenth century in Paris, the cool thing to do was to take a turtle for a walk in the park in order to slow your pace and better appreciate your surroundings.[5] My friend Phil took this idea and made it his own. He decided a few years ago to commit to taking the slow lane for one month. It was an intentional choice to take control of the pace of his life. If he was at the grocery store, he chose the longest line. If he was driving, he took the slowest lane. The only stipulation was that he couldn't use the time he was spending waiting in the slow lane to look at his phone. After thirty days of practicing taking the slow lane, he said his life felt different. He took time to talk to people in line, he wasn't so hurried or anxious, he was happier and kinder, he was having more fun than he'd had in a long time, and even though he was slowing down, he felt like he had more time in his day.

Another helpful way to recalibrate is to unsubscribe from every single email mailing list that doesn't brighten your day. This is super easy. Just scroll to the bottom of the email and look for a small unsubscribe button. Click on it and follow the process. The cacophony of voices that are telling us what we need to buy or do or believe is deafening. So many of the messages we invite into our lives are convincing us that we are unlovable if we don't lose ten pounds, or do the Whole30 for a month, or buy a miracle beauty product. You will not believe how much more you can hear hope and love in your life when you quiet the competing outside voices.

STOP WORRYING AND
START BEING AWED

On a recent episode of my podcast, my guest Harris III, an illusionist and the creative leader of STORY, talked about imagination. He said, "A lot of people think that we lose our imagination when we grow up, but we don't, we just start misusing it. We begin to use our imaginations to dream up every possible thing we should be worrying about, every terrible scenario that might happen."[6] So accurate, right? Our powerful gift of imagination gets misdirected under the guise of being a responsible adult, and what we are left with is fear, worry, and caution instead of fun, awe, and possibility.

A few ways I regain a sense of wonder in my life is to go outside and lie on a blanket to observe the stars, or to visit a place I have never been before. Reconnecting with old friends or going to a concert also sparks those same feelings of awe and possibility for me. When we actively seek out moments that take our breath away, our sense of imagination starts to realign.

My friend Jan decided when she was thirty-three that she was tired of feeling anxious about every detail of her life. She was worried about money, worried about her kids, worried about her husband's job, not to mention worried about her health and whether she was living her best life. One day she decided that, for thirty days, she was going to notice something beautiful that she had never paid attention to before, as a way to retrain her wandering thoughts. What she found is that her thoughts became so consumed with looking for wonder and beauty that she didn't have as much time to worry. After the thirty days she had learned that we see what we are looking for. When we look for wonder, we find it. When we look for worry, we find that too. So we might as well look for what we really want.

STOP MAKING YOURSELF BETTER AND START MAKING OTHERS BETTER

A recent study by Katie Nelson, assistant professor of psychology at Sewanee University, shocked every mental-health expert who was involved in the study's research. The study was focused on finding the factors that determine how happy and content we are as human beings. What the researchers found is that our sense of well-being doesn't come from how other people treat us. It comes from how well we treat other people. Often we convince ourselves that if the people in our lives were more thoughtful or more generous, we would feel happier. But Nelson's research tells us this isn't true. Our sense of well-being comes from how thoughtful and generous *we* are toward *others*:

> "We get these messages from the media telling us that when we want to feel good that we should treat ourselves—that we should go on a shopping trip, we should indulge in a decadent dessert, we should get a massage, get our nails done," Nelson says. "We're constantly told that's a good way to feel good about yourself, and often that's what people do when they want to feel better."[7]

But her research found that engaging in activities that helped other people resulted in more positive emotions and greater well-being, while the people who treated themselves saw no increase in positive emotions and no decrease in negative emotions. Our sense of well-being doesn't require more self-improvement techniques; it requires a little more generosity of spirit.

One way my friend Hank Fortener is teaching his kids

about giving to others, embracing wonder, and owning their uniqueness is by reframing Halloween. Here is what he posted on Instagram:

> My girls keep asking why people are giving them candy at all the parties and why people are handing out candy in every neighborhood. Instead of telling them about All Saints Day and the Celtic tradition of All Hallow's Eve (we will get to that in 1st grade . . .) I told them that Halloween is a night of generosity. I told them that life is better when we give freely with no expectation of return. Especially to strangers. When we give love and kindness and small things (like candy on Halloween) away to everyone in our lives, we make people happy and we are happier too. Like the gift economy of Burning Man, or the communal tradition in scripture that "giving is better than receiving" . . . everything is better when you give. . . . Here's to all the generous people celebrating Halloween, who are giving freely to strangers on their doorsteps and making everything better for all of us.[8]

STOP APOLOGIZING AND START PLAYING

We recently had to deem the s-word a cuss word in our home. And by s-word I mean *sorry*. To be clear, we are big fans of apologizing when you have hurt someone or messed up big time in our family. That is not the *sorry* we are talking about. Let me back up.

One Saturday after a soccer game, my daughter's coach pulled Joe and me aside and said, "I really need your daughter to stop apologizing and start playing." She had scored a goal and immediately apologized to the other team because she didn't want them to feel bad. If she didn't make a perfect pass to a teammate, she apologized. If she bumped up against someone on the field, the first thing out of her mouth was, "I'm sorry." Then her coach said, "She would have so much more fun if she could let herself off the hook from needing to be perfect."

I went home after our sideline intervention from the coach, thinking about the conversation I wanted to have with my girl. As I processed everything I wanted to talk with her about, I realized that the conversation I needed to have with her is the very same thing I and so many of my friends need to hear as well.

So, just for the record, here are things that you do not need to apologize for: trying hard, asking a question, dreaming big, being really good at something, having a curvy body, not having a curvy body, returning something to a store, having a lot of kids, choosing to not have kids. My list could go on and on.

Before her next soccer game, I taped a note to the inside flap of her soccer bag as a fun reminder to show up without apology:

You believed in the tooth fairy for, like, seven years. You can believe in yourself for an hour on the soccer field. You've got this, have some fun. Xoxo

Her team thought it was hilarious. It is still taped to the inside of her bag, and now, a few months later, she has a special dance that includes karate when she scores a goal. So . . . we may be making a little *too much* progress, but we'll take it. In fact, not long ago I overheard her telling her friends that she is having so much more fun playing soccer now.

Here is the takeaway: more fun is available if we stop worrying about all the things we are or aren't. Instead, focus on enjoying the game of life, and make up a little victory dance for when things really go well.

No more making yourself perfect so you can be happy. Be happy so that life will feel a little more perfect. The facts are this: you are floating on a boulder in space, held down by some arbitrary rule of physics that no one can really explain, and spinning around the sun at sixty-seven thousand mph. There's only so much organic material on this planet, meaning it is endlessly recycled. So some part of you was probably part of a dinosaur. For you to exist, every single one of your ancestors had to survive long enough to procreate. Everything is a miracle, and very little is dependent on you, so stop worrying about all the ways you could improve, and start choosing more fun.

A FEW FUN,
NON-SELF-IMPROVEMENT IDEAS

1. Put away your self-help guides and read a novel instead. I would suggest Jane Austen fan fiction, but whatever floats your boat.
2. Take a tango class, because it is fun and super sexy. Boom.
3. Does your posture in the world say "I'm sorry" rather than "I'm killin' it!"? Nothing wrong with showing up to life lit. Watch Amy Cuddy's TED talk called, "Your Body Language May Shape Who You Are."[9]
4. Turn off your phone every day from 9:00 p.m. to 9:00 a.m.
5. Take Phil's "Slow Lane Challenge" or Jan's "Notice Something Beautiful Challenge" for one month.
6. Design your own tattoo.

CHAPTER 9

HAVE MORE FUN
WITH SPIRITUALITY

The more I get to know Jesus, the more trouble
he seems to get me into.

SHANE CLAIBORNE

I was escorted off the property of a church fifteen years
ago because I wouldn't play by the rules (gets me every
time). This means that no matter where you are in your
faith experience today, let me assure you that nothing you
might tell me would be shocking because I have seen it all.

It was spring in Riverside, California, and my husband
Joe and I were youth pastors who wanted to change the
world. We started with a handful of teenagers whose parents brought them to church every Sunday. Joining them
were some neighborhood kids who lived within walking
distance and whose parents had no interest in church but
didn't mind if their kids showed up for donuts. A year into

this gig of caring for kids and their families and building legitimate friendships, the pastor pulled us aside and asked us to stop inviting the teenagers who lived in the low-income housing next door to the church because it made some of the parents of the church kids uncomfortable.

To which we replied, "Come again?" because surely we misheard him. He repeated the same thing we thought we didn't hear the first time. We replied that his request wasn't possible, because we're pretty sure Jesus cares about poor kids too.

And then we were asked to not come back to work, ever.

When we showed up at church the next Sunday to say goodbye, a few men from the congregation quickly approached us, and without saying a word used their bodies to block us from taking a seat in the sanctuary and then looped their arms through ours like we were protesters disturbing the peace and (ahem) *walked* us out to our car, then waited until we drove away to go back into the building.

I was sobbing, Joe was in shock, and to be honest, I am still trying to make sense of it. It took a good three years after that to step foot in a church building again. And if I see anyone from that old church again, I will likely need to tape my sailor mouth shut, so I don't say something that makes Jesus blush.

A few years of therapy have provided me the perspective that sometimes we take ourselves too seriously. Our egos get twisted up with our faith, and we start peddling access to God like bouncers at a nightclub with a velvet rope and a definitive list of who is in and who is out. We equate specific behavior with access to God, which leaves us raw and disillusioned. But if we really understood the message of Jesus, there would be a lot more dancing and celebration and a lot less crying.

HONEST TO GOD

We are going to talk about God in this chapter, and hopefully there is something here that frees you up to be a little more yourself. Because as far as I can tell, there are far too many people feeling like they desperately need more lightness and honesty in their faith, but they aren't quite sure how to dismantle it from stuffy old men and unhelpful rhetoric.

Let's be honest, it might feel unusual to talk about spirituality in a book about having more fun, but it seems to me that so much of our heartache and wandering can be rooted in our search for God and what God expects of us. This is especially important as we begin to remind ourselves that fun is an option, especially in our spiritual lives.

BOTH SONS

There is a story in the Bible written by a doctor named Luke who documented a tale Jesus shared. It is a story that you have probably heard a thousand times before, but I want to take another look at it because there is a sentence that shocks me every time I read it. Here it is:

There was once a man who had two sons. The younger said to his father, "Father, I want right now what's coming to me."

So the father divided the property between them. It wasn't long before the younger son packed his bags and left for a distant country. There, undisciplined and dissipated, he wasted everything he had. After he had gone through all his money, there was a bad famine all through that country and he began to hurt. He signed on with a citizen there who assigned him to his fields to slop the pigs. He was so hungry he would have eaten the corncobs in the pig slop, but no one would give him any.

That brought him to his senses. He said, "All those farmhands working for my father sit down to three meals a day, and here I am starving to death. I'm going back to my father. I'll say to him, Father, I've sinned against God, I've sinned before you; I don't deserve to be called your son. Take me on as a hired hand." He got right up and went home to his father.

When he was still a long way off, his father saw him. His heart pounding, he ran out, embraced him, and kissed him. The son started his speech: "Father, I've sinned against God, I've sinned before you; I don't deserve to be called your son ever again."

But the father wasn't listening. He was calling to the servants, "Quick. Bring a clean set of clothes and dress him. Put the family ring on his finger and sandals on his feet. Then get a grain-fed heifer and roast it. We're going to feast! We're going to have a wonderful time! My son is here—given up for dead and now alive! Given up for lost and now found!" And they began to have a wonderful time.

All this time his older son was out in the field. When the day's work was done he came in. As he approached the house, he heard the music and dancing. Calling over one of the houseboys, he asked what was going on. He told him, "Your brother came home. Your father has ordered a feast—barbecued beef!—because he has him home safe and sound."

The older brother stalked off in an angry sulk and refused to join in. His father came out and tried to talk to him, but he wouldn't listen. The son said, "Look how many years I've stayed here serving you, never giving you one moment of grief, but have you ever thrown a party for me and my friends? Then this son of yours who has thrown away your money on whores shows up and you go all out with a feast!"

His father said, "Son, you don't understand. You're with me all the time, and everything that is mine is yours—but this is a wonderful time, and we had to celebrate. This brother of yours was dead, and he's alive! He was lost, and he's found!" (Luke 15:11–32 MSG)

You have always been with me, and all I have is yours.

I have been both sons. Both were separated from the father, one because of his bad decisions and the other because of his good ones. Both thinking the father's love is dependent on their actions. One believing that all his missteps will result in disappointment or being disowned by the father, the other believing that all his do-gooding is positioning him to earn more of the father's love. How many times are we told that pleasing God is about trying harder?

But the thing that unnerves me the most about this story is that the faithful son has to be told he had access to all of the father's love, joy, and delight, but he was so stuck in his rule-keeping, calloused by spiritual ambition, that he never recognized the celebration. The kingdom of God is like a party—"this is a wonderful time, and we had to celebrate!"—and Jesus has taken care of all the details.

What draws me to Jesus over and over is the simple fact that he offers us a chance to come clean, to stop hustling and pretending we're someone else, and to start again, which seems to me to be a great reason to celebrate. There is nothing we can do to ruin or squander God's love. Equally important, there is also nothing we can do to earn more.

That means the hustling that sucks all the fun out of faith isn't necessary. I wonder if sometimes God is just like, "You guys, this was never meant to be so burdensome. Everyone, slow your roll. Stop defending me on social media and stop obsessing about what elected official is going to pass laws to promote what you think I care about. Stop debating about whether you should make a cake for a wedding, and maybe just show up to the wedding and dance. Bring a present as a gesture that I am good and let me sort out all the issues. You are off duty from policing morality and on duty for having more fun. Love me, love people; all the Law and the Prophets hang on these two commandments."

LIVE ON THE DANCE FLOOR

What would it look like to live on the dance floor of the party? How would it change us to realize we are already with God, and all his goodness and love have been ours the whole time? "You're with me all the time, and everything that is mine is yours." Can you imagine how much more fun we would have? How much more fun we would be? How much freer would we feel? (Side note: have no fear about dancing like no one is watching. Because no one is watching; they are checking their phones. So, dance away.)

For the record, dance-floor spirituality means:

You have a voice. Just in case you are a woman who, at some point in your faith journey, has been made to feel less than or that your voice isn't welcomed, let me remind you of a groundbreaking encounter Jesus had with a woman named Mary in the book written by Luke:

As Jesus and his disciples were on their way, he came to a village where a woman named Martha opened her home to him. She had a sister called Mary, who sat at the Lord's feet listening to what he said. But Martha was distracted by all the preparations that had to be made. She came to him and asked, "Lord, don't you care that my sister has left me to do the work by myself? Tell her to help me!"

"Martha, Martha," the Lord answered, "you are worried and upset about many things, but few things are needed—or indeed only one. Mary has chosen what is better, and it will not be taken away from her." (Luke 10:38–42)

In our Western understanding of this passage, we interpret Martha as the ultimate hostess with the most-est, a busybody who is making sure everyone has had their fill of the charcuterie board and who wouldn't imagine serving refills of lemonade without a rim of lavender-infused sugar on the glass. The narrative we are given is that while Martha is worrying about what shape to cut the sandwiches, her sister Mary is doing what Jesus really wants, which is sitting in his presence.

The problem is that this isn't what the story is about, and it isn't the way the original hearers of this text would have interpreted it. In the context of the first-century world, Martha was merely doing what was normal and expected; she was doing what she should have done when any male had entered her house. The unusual part of the story is that Mary is sitting at the feet of Jesus, which would have made everyone in the room's palms sweat. At that time, sitting at someone's feet meant that he was your rabbi and you were his student, his disciple. And that role was only held by men. #boysclub.

For Mary to forego her expected role as a woman and to be welcomed to sit at the feet of Jesus with the other male disciples meant that Jesus valued a woman's voice and ability to lead others. He was welcoming her into the ranks of the future leaders of the church and the community.

Martha's response, begging Jesus to tell Mary to get up and help her, probably wasn't about Martha being passive-aggressive or having too much work. She was likely worried that Mary would be publicly disgraced for such a bold indiscretion as sitting at a rabbi's feet.[1] Jesus tells Martha that Mary has chosen the better option—accepting God's offer of equality and opportunity over cultural norms to be a disciple, thereby affirming the place of women in the kingdom of God.

Moreover, in a time in history when women couldn't be witnesses in court, God chose women not only to join the ranks of Jesus's successors and students but appointed them as the first witnesses of the resurrection of Jesus. Women were the ones who first preached the gospel. Women are entrusted with an important message and a voice to share it.[2]

You are worthy before you achieve. In the first-century Jewish world, the wilderness wasn't sanctioned, and it was a place where everyone was welcome. When Jesus heads out to the wilderness, he's baptized by John, comes out of the water, and everyone present hears the audible voice of God saying, "This is my Son, whom I love; with him I am well pleased" (Matt. 3:17). Before Jesus does anything fantastic, before he sacrificed, earned, or achieved, he is validated. That's not all. At the same time God affirms his pleasure with Jesus, and a dove hovers over the water. The last time we read about something like that happening was in the Genesis story where God hovers over the waters as creation is taking form. What all of this is telling us is that, with Jesus, there is a new creation, the slate is wiped clean. Jesus in his full humanity is leading us to our full humanity. Without any earning or achieving, we are beloved. This is my child in whom I am well pleased. Calm your racing mind, cease the search for the next best thing. You have always been with him, and all he has is yours.

I get really nervous before I speak to big crowds (and let's be honest, to small crowds, or even before making small talk with just one person or talking on the phone). Regardless, some time ago I was at a mom conference we put on at MOPS called MOMcon.[3] It was the opening night, and I was backstage, sweating through my shirt and hunched over a trash can, heaving the chicken Caesar salad I had for dinner because my stomach felt the nerves most acutely. As I stood there listening to the roar of three thousand women on the other side of the curtain, waiting for me to take the stage, Bob Goff, author of a life-changing book called *Love Does*, steps in front of me, looks me straight in the eye, and says, "I am so proud of you."[4]

Before I had performed or earned any applause, Bob was proud of me, and it changed everything for me in that moment. My shoulders relaxed, the feeling in the pit of my stomach went away, and I had more fun on the stage that night than I ever had before. I hope you have someone in your life who can tell you this, but if not, hear it from me: God is proud of you. I can guess what your inner voice is saying. *Well, what about this, this, and this. God surely isn't proud of those things.* I hear you, but those are part of being human, the part God understands and forgives and sees through.

Have you ever thought about God as fun loving? I have a picture hanging above my desk in my office to remind me that God isn't always angry and disappointed. The picture is of Jesus laughing. It reminds me that Jesus is the person who laughs with us, even as we squander our days looking for something that will open our minds when love and truth are already waiting for us if only we choose to accept it.

Also above my desk is a poem I found in a book called *Love Poems from God* edited by Daniel Ladinsky.[5] The book contains writings from some of the great spiritual thinkers of all time, including Thomas Aquinas and Teresa of Avila. But the piece that stuck out to me most was this poem by Hafiz that I hand wrote on an index card and placed next to laughing Jesus:

> *God and I have become like two giant fat people,*
>   *living on a tiny boat.*
> *We keep bumping into each other and laughing.*
> *Laughing with God. Isn't that great?*[6]

Having more fun with spirituality will show up in your life in different ways, but what I do know is that it typically takes some searching because we only see what we are looking for. It might mean showing up with other people who are looking for the same thing. For me, this sometimes means church, but not always. Jesus is obviously not contained in the church, but he can often be found hanging around in there.

If you are thinking about church, but you feel angry or leery or hurt yet are somehow still drawn to a gathering of people looking for God, I think that is courageous. Also, please know that some people go to church because they believe and others go because they want to believe. Neither is more holy.

Please also know that it is OK for your spiritual journey to be a winding one or for it to look different from those of the people around you. It is also OK to ask questions, to have doubts, and to like Jesus (but not like his people sometimes). We are all doing our best, and God gets it because he lived it too. It was just over two thousand years ago that Jesus was born in a barn to a teenage mom. In a rocky pasture not far from Bethlehem on a hillside speckled with sheep, an angel showed up to a bunch of shepherds, possibly sitting around a campfire and drinking wine out of a skin. The angel said to them, "Do not be afraid; for behold, I bring you good news of great joy which will be for all the people; for today in the city of David there has been born for you a Savior, who is Christ the Lord" (Luke 2:10–11 NASB). One of them surely spat out the wine and whispered, "Was that what I think it was?"

Good news, great joy, for all people. That is Jesus.

ENJOY THE PARTY

One of the greatest compliments I have ever been given was by a homeless woman at a church I belonged to in San Diego. I overheard her inviting a friend from the street to come for donuts, and she said, "I want to introduce you to my friend Mandy. You have to hear how she talks about God." On the other hand, read some of the reviews of my latest book on Amazon and you'll see, "Don't read this book because of the way Mandy talks about God."

I'm not everyone's cup of tea, and it is all good because there is room in the family of God for all of us. All his love, all his forgiveness, and all the hope that one day we will understand entirely. Until then: good news, great joy, for all people. We don't need to see eye to eye to dance hand in hand, so go out and enjoy the party you have been at the whole time.

How do I enjoy the party, you ask? Great question. Here are some ideas to get you started.

Cake as Communion. This is a practice that I bust out occasionally when we need to be reminded of God's goodness. It started when I was a pastor in San Diego, and now I do it once a year at staff prayer time at MOPS. The process is simple. We do the communion reading straight from Scripture, but instead of bread and wine we use cake and whatever beverage we have on hand. Sometimes it is grape juice; if we're at my house, I might substitute champagne. I know this makes some people uncomfortable, but I don't think it needs to. Every day around the world this very same thing happens when church families in other countries "take and eat" with Coca Cola and crackers or whatever makes sense in their cultural context. Taste and see that God is good. It creates just enough dissonance in our minds and taste buds that communion takes on a whole new meaning. The beauty of Jesus's sacrifice at the cross is amplified in our senses, and we are reminded of what a gift it truly is. Try it and let me know what you think.

Embrace Holy Mischief. If you believe Jesus is the bread of life, show it. Take donuts to the director of your local community center to pass out at their after-school program. Knock on doors and offer neighbors loaves of fresh baked bread.

Throw a Blowout Party. Invite the folks who don't get many invitations. Treat them like royalty. Invite the regular partygoers too, making no distinction. Make confetti a priority.

Goff Someone. Find someone who really needs to hear it, and Goff them: look them in the eye and say, "I am so proud of you."

Draw Happy God. Draw the face of a gracious God. Yes, images of God are fraught with complication. Even more so if you're not a gifted artist. But you could scribble out a smiley face that represents God's joy. Then put it on the fridge.

Post-its. Leave Post-it notes with encouraging messages around town in random places.

CHAPTER 10

HAVE MORE FUN CHANGING THE WORLD

Just don't give up trying to do what you really want to do. Where there is love and inspiration, I don't think you can go wrong.

ELLA FITZGERALD

It all started with a mom none of us have heard of, and a note she wrote to her son.

It's the summer of 1920, and arguably the hottest month in decades in Nashville, Tennessee. The Hermitage Hotel downtown is packed to the brim with legislators, lawyers, journalists, and women who have traveled for miles, and everyone is wearing a rose on their collar, which is how they know who to talk to. Tension is high, and the humidity clogs every room with the smell of cigarette smoke, making it hard to breathe.

About forty years earlier, Congress had voted on the

Fourteenth Amendment, giving slaves the right to vote. As the amendment was drafted, many women across the States were convinced this was the moment in history when all forms of discrimination—including those against women—would be dismantled from the Constitution. But, at the very last minute before the official vote, the word *male* was added to the amendment. Women, again, were denied the right to vote.

Forty years later, on June 4, 1919, Congress voted to add thirty-nine words to the Constitution. These thirty-nine simple words, also known as the Nineteenth Amendment, would give women the right to vote. There was only one catch: thirty-six states (out of forty-eight at the time) had to approve it.

Eleven states quickly ratified the amendment within the first month, and twenty-four more steadily voted their approval over the next nine months. But then support stalled, and five months passed with no more votes and none of the remaining states likely to vote in favor of it.

Until, Tennessee. Which takes us back to the Hermitage Hotel and the lawyers, legislators, and women who had descended on Nashville. Everyone was wearing a rose on their lapel very intentionally. Those wearing a yellow rose supported women's right to vote; those wearing a red rose were against it.

On the morning of August 18, 1920, the hotel began clearing out as legislators made their way to Union Station, where the final vote was going to be held. Having counted the roses that morning, the suffragettes knew they were in trouble. In fact, Carrie Chapman Catt, the leader of the suffragettes, decided to stay behind at the hotel, telling her friends that there was only one thing they could now do: "We can pray."[1]

Meanwhile, a few blocks from the Hermitage Hotel at Union Station, ninety-nine legislators shifted in their seats, fanning themselves with paper, wilted roses on their collars. One by one the men stood up to vote. Those with a yellow rose said *aye* in support of women's right to vote, and those wearing red replied with *nay*. The vote proceeded until it was Harry Burn's turn. Harry T. Burn, from Niota, Tennessee, was the youngest legislator in the house. Small in stature and serious in disposition, Harry blended into the background, never one to make a scene. Harry stood to cast his vote, wearing a red rose in his lapel. But in his pocket was a letter he had just received from his mother, back home in Niota.

Febb Burn had sent her son an ordinary letter that any other mother might have written. It was filled with details about the family farm and updates on the neighbors, but tucked into those mundane details about life in Niota were these words:

> Dear Son, ... Hurrah and vote for suffrage and don't keep them in doubt. . . . I've been watching to see how you stood but have not seen anything yet. . . .

Don't forget to be a good boy, and help Mrs. "Thomas
Catt.". . . . With lots of love, Mama[2]

Harry voted "aye."

Everyone was silent; they couldn't believe what just
happened. Harry changed his vote. The final tally: 49 to 47.

Chaos erupted. Legend has it that the anti-suffragettes
were so livid they chased Harry right out of the building,
and he had to jump out a window and hide in the capital
library until the fury died down.

Six days later, the Nineteenth Amendment became
national law.[3] And now you and I have the right to vote
because Febb Burn sent her son a note. Isn't that fun?

I love this story, because who doesn't love a bunch of
angry government officials chasing down one of their own
until he has to jump out a window and hide in a library?
But the bigger reason is because the most remarkable part
of this story has nothing to do with politics. It is the fact
that moms can change the future simply by living their
everyday lives.

So often women—particularly moms—feel stuck or
stifled by the demands of their lives. Nearly every woman
I know has a deep longing to find her God-given passion
and purpose and to feel that she is doing something meaningful in the world. But not many of us know how to start.
Additionally, we have the pressure to do this meaningful
thing alongside everything else we are managing, and to
do it in such a way that it changes the world.

But what does changing the world really mean? I would argue it means something different than we think it does.

DON'T CHANGE THE WORLD

I sometimes wonder if we might benefit from a new perspective on what it means to change the world, because it is a fairly recent concept in the grand scheme of history. My friend Jared Mackey did some research on the number of books with "change the world" in the title over time, and here is what he found:

Before 1900: 0
1900–1950: 4
1950–1980: 12
1980–2000: 101
2000–2018: 20,000+

Only within the last twenty years did we start assuming that part of our God-given purpose was to do something so big that it would impact the whole world. Now everyone is obsessed with changing the world, but nobody wants to change the toilet paper roll. The problem is, I don't think this is healthy. It seems that this pressure to do something big is contributing to the sky-rocketing rates of anxiety that we are experiencing as a generation of women. No longer can we live well, care for our neighbors, and raise our kids. Now we have to change the whole entire world at the same time.

What if God's big plan for our lives is that we wouldn't spend so much time trying to figure out a big plan for our lives? Maybe purpose doesn't come in chasing down the extraordinary. Febb Burn influenced an entire nation by simply writing her son a note. What if we changed our focus from feeling the pressure of changing the world to just changing our small part of the world?

Below are some ways that some really cool people are changing their worlds.

The Midtown Games

My friend Zefrey Throwell is an artist and social commentator in Midtown, New York, who is constantly looking for new ways to change his world. After realizing that Midtown is the most hated neighborhood in New York City, he and some friends coordinated what they called the Midtown Games as a fun way to help New Yorkers reclaim that part of town. A little after noon on September 29, 2011, as office workers flooded the sidewalks, Zefrey and more than one hundred friends staged an office-worker Olympics with events like the 50-meter swim held in a fountain near Rockefeller Center, a ping-pong game with more than fifty players, a 100-meter dash along the Avenue of the Americas, and a 250-meter relay through Times Square. Bystanders were encouraged to join in the fun. News of the Midtown Games spread quickly, and people in nearby skyscrapers were soon pouring out the front doors of their buildings to come and see what was going on. It was a day of fun and levity for all who witnessed it. Midtown is still not a favorite of many New Yorkers, but that day everyone who witnessed the Midtown Games experienced a world that was a little more fun because Zefrey declared it was so.

A Five-Course Dinner with New Friends

A group of my friends decided to throw a dinner party for women who needed a reminder that they are loved and worthy. On a Tuesday night they walked through downtown Denver and asked five women what their rate was for the whole night. Then they paid them their rates and told them that they were free to head home, but if they were willing, they'd love to take them to dinner.

Earlier in the day, they had set up a beautiful dinner in a nearby restaurant. There were flowers and white linens and china plates. There was an elaborate five-course meal, and at each place setting there was a handwritten note that said, "Just a reminder, you are loved, you are worthy, you are beloved." My friends lingered around a table with five new friends, each of whom had a reprieve from selling her body that night. There was laughter, story sharing, and tears. My friends reminded them that they are deeply loved by a good God. At the end of the evening, everyone agreed it was a night of fun, nourishment, and hope. They all hugged, and many of the women went home to be with their kids, who were usually by themselves while their moms worked all night. They weren't disentangled forever from selling their bodies, but it changed their world for a night. And who knows where that will lead them next.

Celebrate through the Bad Moments Too

Last year I was at a women's event with singer JJ Heller in Pennsylvania, and a woman told me about an unusual neighborhood celebration she'd just experienced. One of her longtime neighbors and dearest friends had been laid off from a company he had worked at for more than twenty-six years. It was a devastating blow to his ego, and his neighborhood friends wanted to find a way to cheer him up and have fun despite horrible circumstances. So on his last day of work, his neighbors held a "graduation" party for him. They lined his street at 5:00 p.m. with balloons and loud music, and as he drove home from his last day at that office they held up signs celebrating the fact that he was graduating onto something new. They partied in their cul-de-sac late into the evening, and he later said it was the best, worst moment he ever had. The day his world changed was the day his neighbors showed up to celebrate.

Notes to Strangers

Two years ago at MOPS, we launched a campaign to leave love letters for random strangers to find. The idea was that sometimes as a mom it is difficult to feel like you have the time or energy to do anything meaningful in the world (oh, other than, say, raising the next generation of humans on this planet). So we rallied moms to sit for a moment, think about the people who might find the notes they were writing, and then to ask God for a message for each of those people. More than one hundred thousand moms participated, writing notes to random people and leaving them in public places for strangers to find. It was crazy fun to watch the stories come in from people who found the notes at bus stops, in grocery carts, on the subway, and at playgrounds. What we heard over and over was how finding a letter changed that person's world that day so that suddenly the thing they were worried about felt a little more bearable, simply because a note that a stranger wrote found its way to them.

Start with the Moms

In 2012, Colombia was still embroiled in a fifty-two-year-long civil war, the longest running conflict in the western hemisphere. The Revolutionary Armed Forces of Colombia, also known as FARC, had been attempting to overthrow the government. There were at least 220,000 dead and millions displaced. With no sign of resolution, Colombia's Ministry of Defense decided that they needed to get more creative to try to bring peace to the country. They came up with one of the most unusual ideas in modern warfare: an advertising campaign. They hired a creative ad executive and native Colombian, Jose Miguel

Sokoloff, to convince thousands of rebel fighters to give up without firing a shot. How did he do it? Moms.

His team created a series of advertising campaigns to convince the guerrillas to surrender and to simultaneously convince the Colombian people to accept them back into normal life. The only problem was that the guerrillas were scattered throughout 175,000 dense acres of jungle. So they got creative and called in the rebels' moms.

The ad campaign included thirty moms whose children had run away to fight. They shared photos of their missing kids, and Sokoloff and his team made them into posters with a message from their mom that read, "Before you were a guerrilla, you were my son. Come home because I am waiting for you." Some of the moms had been waiting for twenty years. After seeing messages from their moms, nearly three-hundred guerrillas came out of the jungle and gave up. It has been the most successful peacemaking effort Colombia has experienced. Moms changed their world by loving their kids and reminding them that no matter what they had done, they could come home.

KEEP GOING AND WEAR LIPSTICK

According to the Smithsonian Institute, women have been wearing lipstick for nearly six thousand years. From crushing semiprecious jewels into powder or mixing fish scales with castor oil and beeswax, women have been

using ingenuity and resourcefulness to enhance everything around them ever since the beginning of time.

And while there are those who would argue that lipstick is simply a vain pursuit meant to bring out a woman's
beauty or attract the opposite sex, I couldn't disagree more.
For centuries, lipstick has been a vehicle of empowerment,
a mark of courage, and from my vantage point lipstick is
war paint.

If you don't believe me take it from Kathrine Switzer.

Kathrine Switzer loves to run. Not only does she love
to run, she loves to run marathons. For those of us that
don't enjoy literal pain as a hobby, the length of a marathon is 26.2 miles, otherwise known as a miniature road
trip. But to Kathrine, 26.2 miles is simply a fun way to
spend a few hours.

Between the ages of twenty and sixty-five, Kathrine
ran thirty-nine marathons and ended up changing the
course of history on one cold and snowy day in 1967 . . .
but that is jumping ahead. Let's start at the beginning.

Growing up, Kathrine loved sports, loved competing,
and loved keeping up with the boys. Her impressive athlet-
icism as a girl was hard for some people to make sense of
and even harder to figure out what to do with. Growing up
in the 1960s didn't provide a lot of opportunities for a girl
to capitalize on her love of running. In fact, it was a com-
monly held belief that women were too weak to run long
distances; so, the thought of a woman running a marathon
was not only absurd but against every unspoken rule.

While young men were being awarded college scholarships and Olympic opportunities for their long-distance prowess, girls were told that they were physically incapable of competing in such a rigorous race.

But Kathrine kept running.

After being accepted to Syracuse University for college, she began unofficially practicing with the men's cross-country team since there was no women's running team there, or anywhere else in the country at the time.

One snowy night in December 1966, while nineteen-year-old Kathrine was running her nightly ten miles, Arnie, a fifty-year-old coach and trainer at the university, joined her for a run. Arnie was recounting stories of his annual participation in the mecca for all male runners, the Boston Marathon (I know what you're thinking: How does one have a conversation while running ten miles? Apparently, it is possible). After hearing his tales of endurance and accomplishment, Kathrine responded, "Oh, let's quit talking about the Boston Marathon and run the damn thing!"

"Women can't run the Boston Marathon," Arnie responded.

"Why not? I'm running ten miles a night!" Kathrine fired back.

"No dame has ever run the Boston Marathon!"

Yet Arnie made a deal with her. If she could run the distance in practice, he would take her to Boston.

Just a couple months later, she ran the 26.2 miles in practice and then decided to run five more miles just for good measure.

Her fate was sealed.

Kathrine registered for the race, signing her name K. V. Switzer and plunking down the $3 entry fee. A few weeks later, joined by a couple of other guys on the Syracuse cross-country team, Kathrine, her coach Arnie, and her running friends headed to Boston for the big event. The marathon started at noon on April 19, 1967. As she walked through the crowd of runners, there were a lot of double takes and "good-for-you"s, and overall she felt very welcomed by the other men who were stretching and warming up for the race.

Right before reaching the starting line, one of her teammates looked at her and said, "You're wearing lipstick!?"

"I always wear lipstick. What's wrong with that?"

"Somebody might see you are a girl and not let you run. Take it off."

In epic Kathrine fashion, she responded, "I will not take off my lipstick." (Preach.)

And that's how she began the race.

When the gun went off at the starting line, 740 men and one woman began the marathon. Just a few miles in, a press truck pulled up beside her, and news stations began taking photos of the spectacle that was a woman running the Boston Marathon.

What happened next sent her into a whirlwind of adrenaline and confusion. A man in a suit hopped off the press truck and stormed toward her, yanking at her shoulder and screaming at her to "get the h*ll out of my race!" Her mind could not register what was taking place. *His race!*

He continued to claw at her, trying to remove her from the race by any means possible, viciously grabbing at her shirt and bib number. As it turns out, the man attacking her was the race manager, a man by the name of Jock Semple (You can't make this stuff up. Jock!). As she struggled to keep running while he manhandled her, she had never felt so much embarrassment or fear in her life. Finally, one of her friends from Syracuse tackled him off of her, sending him to the ground.

Dazed and confused, and not knowing what else to do, Arnie her coach yelled out "run like h*ll," and she did. Kathrine and her friends picked up the pace. Her first thought was that her teammate had killed the manager of the race with his forceful shove. And for half a second, she thought about quitting. But then it slowly began to sink in that no matter what, she had to finish this race, even if she had to crawl across the finish line. Even if ten more Jock Semples attacked her. Even if Arnie and the other men she came with couldn't associate with her anymore because of ramifications from the Amateur Athletic Union.

She knew that if she didn't finish, people would say it is because women can't do it. She knew that her actions in that very moment would determine one of two things: forward movement or backward progress. Nothing in between.

Kathrine had something to prove, but not to herself—to the world. She was no longer running on behalf of herself but on behalf of all women.

Fully expecting to be arrested by the organizers of the race, Kathrine kept running as snow fell from the sky and blisters formed on her feet and the press ridiculed her from the sidelines. I guess that's the thing about endurance—it demands blood, sweat, and tears. It demands these things because it deeply matters. Endurance demands we abandon the path of least resistance. If I were Kathrine, I would have wanted to flip the manager the bird, quit the race, soak my bloody feet, and hide in the comfort of my mom's arms. And maybe Kathrine wanted to do those things, but she resisted the urge, because there was far too much at stake.

So forward she ran. Red on her bloody socks, red in her eyes, and red on her lips, she endured. Blood, sweat, and lipstick. Kathrine Switzer became the first woman to officially finish the Boston Marathon and changed history as we know it, and she says she had fun doing it.

You can too.

Put on some red lipstick and get to it.

I hope you're starting to see it by now: you have so much capacity and creativity to make change happen! Are you ready to get started changing your world?

SOME WAYS TO HAVE MORE FUN CHANGING YOUR WORLD

1. Buy cans of soda and bottled water and put them on ice in a big cooler. Then set up at a local intersection or exercise trail to give them away!

2. Want to change the whole world for another living being? Adopt an animal from a shelter. It will be one of the most life-giving offerings you can do to change that animal's world and yours.

3. Set up a pop-up listening booth in your local park.[4]

4. Get a big roll of banner paper, create a "honk if you love [insert your friend's name here]" sign, and tape it to their front porch. (Obviously, honk a lot too.)

5. Know a single mom? An overworked, married one? Offer to read bedtime stories to her kids while she unwinds with a glass of wine.

6. Write a real, physical letter to someone without robust relationships.

7. Friends with a mom who has a child with a disability? Give her a night out, while you play games and watch movies with her cool kid.

8. Go chalking. When a friend or neighbor is going through a hard time or celebrating something special, go to their house at night and draw pictures and write fun, encouraging messages all over their sidewalk or driveway, using sidewalk chalk.

CONCLUSION

In May 1952, my nana made a cake that had bubblegum frosting: chewable, blow-a-bubble-with-it frosting. No one has been able to replicate it since. It is the stuff of legends, but it didn't start out that way.

My mom was turning two, and as tradition warranted, my nana (her grandma) offered to make a birthday cake to celebrate. The plan was to mix up some vanilla sponge cake and then layer and cover it with pink frosting. The oven was heated to 375°F, and the cake cooked for twenty-five minutes. During that time, Nana whipped up her classic fondant recipe with a generous amount of powdered sugar, butter, and a splash of milk. As Nana combined ingredients, kids ran in and out of the kitchen, aunties who had arrived early to help set up for the party popped in asking where tablecloths were, and the happy chaos of party preparations buzzed around her.

Sometime in the middle of all the distractions, ingredients were combined in an inexact way, and when it came time to frost the cake, the pink buttery frosting was a little thicker than usual. With only a few minutes to spare before guests started to arrive, Nana didn't waste any time pondering why the texture of the frosting was different. She simply made the cake pretty and put it in the fridge until it was time to sing "Happy Birthday" and blow out the candles.

A few hours into the party, Nana's cake was presented to the crowd, candles lit. A wish was made, and cake made its way into the hands of family and friends who had come to celebrate. The first adult to take a bite of the cake spit out the frosting, claiming it was too chewy. My nana, hearing the comment, took a bite herself, mortified that her frosting had turned out so terribly chewy. She quickly began gathering plates that had been passed out in hopes of sparing guests who hadn't tried it yet from the disgusting frosting faux paus.

But something remarkable happened as the kids took bites. Delirium ensued as they discovered that this cake had bubblegum frosting. It was a dream come true. They started to blow bubbles with it, and the adults, seeing their excitement, had a new appreciation for the chewy frosting. Adults and kids alike were soon marveling at a cake unlike anything they had ever tried before. My nana was a genius, and they all requested a bubblegum cake for their next birthday party. Humiliation turned to delight, and there was more laughing and wonder than had ever been experienced at any birthday party prior.

After trying unsuccessfully for years to replicate the recipe, the legend of the bubblegum-frosting cake has been archived as family lore, passed down from generation to generation, earning its reputation as the best birthday cake ever. It also evokes the same response from every kid who hears the story, without fail, he or she requests a bubblegum cake for their next birthday. Mistake becomes legend. A simple moment of family fun turns into a future story of hope and whimsy for years to come. Fun makes big ripples.

This is why I am committed to making a case for having a really good time. Life is short, too short to spend our time dwelling on mistakes or what we don't have. Too short to feel like a shell of a human being, going through the motions but never really living. The good news is that even when you feel bone tired, dead inside, or like you're holding your breath, you can come back to life. It's time to regain your aliveness.

WHEN YOUR BONES ARE DRY

Ezekiel was a regular guy whose supernatural vision landed him in the annals of history when he found himself in the middle of a valley, ankle deep in sun-bleached skeletons. Bones are mixed helter-skelter across the wind-whipped sand, a fibula here, a scapula there. Then, as Ezekiel began to speak truth and hope over the bones, reminding them what God says to them, the rattling of bone against bone starts reverberating so forcefully Ezekiel can feel it in his chest. Suddenly, drawn by an unseen magnet, bones are pulled back to their original partners as God begins the process of restoring all the things that at first glance appeared hopeless and lifeless. Bodies are reassembled, and breath returns; the bones once again house souls, and a mighty army of people become warriors of hope. They regain their aliveness. Here is how it goes down:

> I saw a great many bones on the floor of the valley, bones that were very dry. He asked me, "Son of man, can these bones live?" I said, "Sovereign LORD, you alone know."
>
> Then he said to me, "Prophesy to these bones and say to them, 'Dry bones, hear the word of the LORD! This is what the Sovereign LORD says to these bones: I will make breath enter you, and you will come to life. I will attach tendons to you and make flesh come upon you and cover you with skin; I will put breath in you, and you will come to life. Then you will know that I am the LORD.'"
>
> So I prophesied as I was commanded. And as I was prophesying, there was a noise, a rattling sound, and the bones came together, bone to bone. I looked, and tendons and flesh appeared on them and skin covered them, but there was no breath in them.
>
> Then he said to me, "Prophesy to the breath;

prophesy, son of man, and say to it, 'This is what the Sovereign LORD says: Come, breath, from the four winds and breathe into these slain, that they may live.'" So I prophesied as he commanded me, and breath entered them; they came to life and stood up on their feet—a vast army. (Ezekiel 37:2–10)

This story starts with Ezekiel, but the message is ultimately a glimpse into the future, meant to give the people of Israel hope that there was life ahead of them despite their exile. By this time in history, the ten tribes of Israel were so widely scattered among the surrounding nations that they felt utterly lost. The other two tribes had recently been carried away captive to Babylon. It looked as if they would never again return to the promised land. While this unusual story of bones coming back to life began as a promise for the restoration of the entire nation of Israel, it is also a promise for us.

Most of us do a pretty good job of covering up our dry bones. Maybe our marriages are dry and barren. Or maybe there has been a loss of vitality in our bodies. Some of us have bank accounts that are like dry bones. Whatever the cause of our dry bones, God is in the business of bringing dead things back to life and doing the impossible. Sometimes this holy restoration happens miraculously, but other times it happens because you randomly picked up a book about fun and decided it's time to come to life and start choosing joy.

A frequently overlooked part of the story of the dry bones is that at the end, the revived bones become an army that is charged to fight for life in all its fullness. I like this image of an army, and it feels apropos that with all of us, a generation of women coming back to life, we would be a formidable force. Women who reject the lie that we do not have a choice. Women who fight for fullness of life not only for ourselves but for others, women who are flinging open the doors of the stalls we find ourselves in. Women who are making fun and bringing hope everywhere our feet take us.

Whereas armies typically wage war, we wage fun. Our battle cry is ringing loud.

Now, hear this good news! This is what God says: breath is filling your lungs, and you are coming to life. Your heart is beating, your skin is feeling, you are pulsing with aliveness. Come, breath, from the four winds and breathe hope.

Arise and have more fun.

Amen. Let it be so.

ACKNOWLEDGMENTS

To my teammates at MOPS, I couldn't be more thankful to get to spend my days alongside you. Thanks for the pranks, the inspiration, and for caring so deeply about the work we are all called to: Amy Cooper, Andrea Jones, Bethany Clarkson, Chelsea Robbins, Chris Ulshoffer, Cristina Cardoso, Danica Golden, Dawn Hempel, Deidre Hamilton, Elizabeth Billups, Emma Turnbull, Erica Krysl, Gayle Wright, Greg Henry, Hannah Hladek, Hayelom Reda, Jamie Mertens, Janella Thaxton, Janna Sharp, Jennifer Evans, Jennifer Iverson, Jennifer Martin, Jinny Jordan, Keith Becker, Kelli Jordan, Kelli Smith, Kevin McMahon, Kim Garrett, Laura Tate, Lisa Trujillo, Marilee Belote, Matthew Marrs, Matthew Crawford, Melodi Leih, Michelle Flaherty, Moria Cox, Sarah Fraser, Sherri Crandall, Tamara Ordonez, Tanya Rodriguez, TJ Rikli, Todd Stuart, and Tracy Ro.

To the MOPS board of directors, your wisdom and guidance have made me a better leader. Thank you for your patience, kindness, and passion for the mission of MOPS: Cathy Penshorn, Cathy Roberts, Carol O'Leary, Derozette Banks, Ed Ollie, Greg Bowlin, Jeanne McMains, Keith McVaney, Kim Laydon, Kneeland Brown, Makiko Harrison, Nichole Tautz, Pamela Christian, Tracey Solomon, and Yvette Maher.

To Amanda Cant: My right-hand person. Thank you for your thoughtfulness, for managing all the details, and for the notes when I travel. You bring laughter, tenacity, and energy to every room you enter, and that is a huge gift to all of us who get to be in your presence.

To Stephanie Smith, Chris Beetham, Bridgette Brooks, and Robin Barnett: my incredible team at Zondervan. Thank you for the opportunity to write and for walking me through each step with gentleness and honesty. Being able to put a book out into the world is a privilege I will forever appreciate.

To Margot Starbuck: for your help and encouragement when I didn't think I could do it. You are funny, wise, unique, and made every part of this book better.

To Gramps: for passing down good genes, a fierce sense of humor, a zest for life, in addition to a love for words, music, and the stage. I want to be like you when I grow up.

To Mom: for everything. For being the best mom a kid could ask for, for loving us so unconditionally, for being brave with your story, for modeling how to be a good friend, and for letting us have adventures.

To Charley Lacey, CJ, and Mckinley: for teaching my kids

all the things that I can't as their mom. Thank you for all the times around mom's kitchen table, laughing and telling stories late into the night. Also, it's time to move to Colorado.

To Joseph: my lionhearted firstborn. You are tender and tough, a leader of leaders. I respect you and am so proud to be your mom. You are hardworking, funny, and a fashion trendsetter. Thanks for filling our house with music. You have all my love always. P.S. You are never too old for me to bear-hug you.

To Elle: ever since you were a baby, you have been fearless and independent. You have a charisma that others are drawn to, a confidence that allows you to talk to anyone about anything, and a love for life that is contagious. You have a gift for making spaces beautiful, and I am sure that your prowess for writing will one day mean I get to read a book you have written. Be courageous in using your words and voice, because you have important things to say. Also, please take me on your adventures around the world. I love you forever.

To Charlotte: you are masterful at gathering friends, and where you go others want to follow. You are the best salesperson I have ever met, a talented athlete, and an excellent snuggler. Your smile brightens up every room you enter, and favor goes before you. Goodnight, thank you, I love you. Also, promise you will never get too cool to watch Hallmark movies with me.

To Joe: thank you for living real life with me. For reminding me to have fun and for being the best Dad to our kids. I am lucky to be yours.

NOTES

Introduction

1. Corine Gatti, "6 Ways to Renew Yourself This Summer," beliefnet, http://www.beliefnet.com/inspiration/6-ways -to-renew-yourself-this-summer.aspx.
2. "You Have 30,000 Days to Live," Elite Daily, 28 June 2013, https://www.elitedaily.com/life/you-have-30000-days-to-live.

Chapter 1: When You Forget to Have Fun

1. H. L. Mencken, *A Mencken Chrestomathy: His Own Selection of His Choicest Writings* (Knopf: New York, 1949; repr., First Vintage, 1982), 624.
2. Richard Rohr, *Falling Upward* (San Francisco: Jossey-Bass, 2011), 44–45.

Chapter 2: Have More Fun with Friendship

1. Amy Poehler, *Yes, Please* (New York: Dey Street, 2014), 32.

Chapter 3: Have More Fun with Parenting

1. Here is the deal. Some of you will see Rob Bell's name and automatically put this book down. I think that

is a total bummer because he has great ideas about parenting that have nothing to do with theology. I also think we can agree about some things and disagree on others and still be friends. Rob Bell, *Launching Rockets: 17 Observations on Being a Parent* (self-published, 2018), https://robbell.com/portfolio/launching-rockets-17-observations-on-being-a-parent.

2. Subscribe to Hank's podcast, *Hank Presents*, found at https://soundcloud.com/hankfortener. This story comes from the "Live! Mother's Day" episode. Also check out the work Hank is doing to help families fundraise for adoption at www.adopttogether.org.

Chapter 4: Have More Fun in Your Body

1. Goran Blazeski, "The Bizarre Practice of Foot-Binding Was Once a Symbol of Beauty in China," the vintage news.com, 10 December 2017, https://www.thevintage news.com/2017/12/10/foot-binding/.

2. Elizabeth Gilbert, *Big Magic: Creative Living beyond Fear* (New York: Riverhead, 2015), 119.

3. David Whyte, "Sweet Darkness," from *River Flow: New & Selected Poems*, rev. ed. (Langley, WA: Many Rivers, 2012), 348.

4. Kristine Neeley, Instagram, February 25, 2018, www.insta gram.com/p/Bfo_k4KBxMx/?hl=en&taken-by=kristineneeley.

5. The entire story can be found in Mark 5:21–43.

6. The story can be found in John 21:1–14.

7. The account can be found in 1 Kings 18:16–19:9.

8. Olga Khazan, "For Depression, Prescribing Exercise before Medication," *The Atlantic*, 24 March 2014, www.theatlantic.com/health/archive/2014/03/for-depression-prescribing-exercise-before-medication/284587/.

9. Humans of New York, Instagram, August 9, 2017, www
   .instagram.com/p/BXlj-uTgRHl/?utm_source=ig_embed.

Chapter 5: Have More Fun with Sex and Marriage

1. This is a lesson we learned from our friend Amena
   Brown. You can read more in her book *How to Fix a
   Broken Record* (Grand Rapids: Zondervan, 2017), or listen
   to my podcast interview with her at www.mandyarioto
   .com/podcast/2018/2/13/how-to-fix-a-broken-record.
2. You can hear this story on Mike Rowe's podcast called *The
   Way I Heard It*. Listen to episode seven, "Be Right Back,
   Hon!," 08 March 2016, http://mikerowe.com/podcast/.
3. In case you are interested, you can see the pictures in
   my Facebook photos. You'll need to scroll down through
   several years of photos, which prove we have made fun a
   priority ever since.

Chapter 6: Have More Fun When Things Don't Go as Planned

1. Dan Gilbert, "The Surprising Science of Happiness,"
   TED2004, February 2004, www.ted.com/talks/dan
   _gilbert_asks_why_are_we_happy.
2. Dan Gilbert, "The Surprising Science of Happiness,"
   TED2004, https://www.ted.com/talks/dan_gilbert_asks
   _why_are_we_happy/transcript#t-717156.

Chapter 7: Have More Fun with Work

1. Theodore Roosevelt, *The Autobiography of Theodore
   Roosevelt* (Charles Scribner's Sons, 1920; repr., Seven
   Treasures, 2009), 73.
2. Theodore Roosevelt, *A Book-Lover's Holiday in the
   Open* (New York: Charle'1916), foreword.

3. "Algonquin, Teddy Roosevelt's Son's Pony," Presidential Pet Museum, 22 July 2013, http://www.presidentialpet museum.com/pets/algonquin/.

4. Brad Nehring, "4 True Stories That Prove Teddy Roosevelt Was the Toughest Person Ever," The Clymb, http://blog.theclymb.com/out-there/4-true-stories-prove-teddy-roosevelt-toughest-person-ever/.

5. "Theodore Roosevelt's Amazing List of Firsts," Kids Discover, March 28, 2014, https://www.kidsdiscover .com/quick-reads/theodore-roosevelts-amazing-list-firsts/.

6. Chip Heath and Dan Heath, *The Power of Moments: Why Certain Experiences Have Extraordinary Impact* (New York: Simon & Schuster, 2017).

7. Rachel Hollis, Instagram, May 21, 2018, https://www .instagram.com/p/BjDBCNfhsYe/.

Chapter 8: Have More Fun with Self-Improvement

1. Alexandra Schwartz, "Improving Ourselves to Death," *The New Yorker*, January 15, 2018, https://www.new yorker.com/magazine/2018/01/15/improving-ourselves -to-death.

2. Ibid.

3. Leeana Tankersley, *Begin Again: The Brave Practice of Releasing Hurt and Receiving Rest* (Grand Rapids: Revell, 2018), 135–36.

4. "Americans Check Their Phones 80 Times a Day: Study," *New York Post*, November 8, 2017, https://nypost .com/2017/11/08/americans-check-their-phones-80-times -a-day-study/.

5. Richard Prouty, "A Turtle on a Leash," *One-Way Street*, October 28, 2009, onewaystreet.typepad.com/one_way_ street/2009/10/a-turtle-on-a-leash.html.

6. "Harris III—Being Weird and Telling Good Stories," May 28, 2018, http://www.mandyarioto.com/podcast/.

7. Buck Butler, "Prescription for Happiness," Sewanee: The University of the South, www.sewanee.edu/features/ story/happiness.html.

8. Hank Fortener, Instagram, October 29, 2017, www.insta gram.com/p/Ba1wpiHnOmL/?hl=en&taken-by=hank.

9. Amy Cuddy, "Your Body Language May Shape Who You Are," TEDGlobal 2012, June 2012, www.ted.com/talks/ amy_cuddy_your_body_language_shapes_who_you_are.

Chapter 9: Have More Fun with Spirituality

1. Cf. Barbara Leonhard, "Jesus' Extraordinary Treatment of Women," franciscanmedia.org, www.franciscanmedia. org/jesus-extraordinary-treatment-of-women/.

2. Carolyn Custis James has written extensively on this topic. I highly recommend her books *Lost Women of the Bible: The Women We Thought We Knew* (Grand Rapids: Zondervan, 2008) and *Half the Church: Recapturing God's Global Vision for Women* (Grand Rapids: Zondervan, 2015).

3. The largest mom conference in the world. Held every fall, it is the kind of weekend that you need to experience at least once. Find out more at www.mops.org.

4. Bob Goff is one inspiring dude. Learn more about him at bobgoff.com, and check out his newest book *Everybody Always: Becoming Love in a World Full of Setbacks and Difficult People* (Nashville: Nelson, 2018). I also did a podcast with him and his wife entitled "An Interview with Bob and Maria Goff: How to Live a Life of Whimsy, Meaning, and Legacy," February 5, 2018. You can find it at www.mandyarioto.com/podcast/2018/2/5/how-to-live -a-life-of-whimsy-meaning-and-legacy.

5. *Love Poems from God: Twelve Sacred Voices from the East and West* (New York: Penguin Compass, 2002).

6. *Love Poems from God*, 171.

Chapter 10: Have More Fun Changing the World

1. The Tennessee State Museum, "Showdown in Nashville," Tennessee4me, www.tn4me.org/article.cfm/era_id/6/major_id/20/minor_id/56/a_id/136.

2. East Tennessee Historical Society, "'Don't Forget to Be a Good Boy': Harry T. Burn's Letter from Mom and the Ratification of the 19th Amendment in Tennessee," Teach Tennessee History, http://www.teachtnhistory.org/File/Harry_T._Burn.pdf. The document includes a scan of the actual letter sent by Febb Burn to her son Harry.

3. Latif Nasser, "One Vote," *Radiolab*, November 7, 2016, www.radiolab.org/story/one-vote/.

4. Not sure what a listening booth is? See Stephen Giles, "What I've Learned from Hosting the Listening Booth," Spark Monument Circle, August 26, 2015, http://circles park.org/what-ive-learned-from-hosting-the-listening -booth-at-spark/.

Starry-Eyed

Seeing Grace in the Unfolding Constellation of Life and Motherhood

Mandy Arioto

Find Grace and Meaning amid Motherhood's Highs and Lows

Being a mom is all of it: light and dark, highs and lows, fever-pitch frustration and all-consuming love. By now, you already know that with great love comes great joy . . . and great pain. It can be crazy making! But it doesn't have to be.

In *Starry-Eyed*, MOPS CEO Mandy Arioto reveals how the brightest and darkest moments of motherhood alike can become a sacred—and sanity-saving—opportunity to encounter God. There is a way to flourish in the midst of it all, and it starts with embracing the light and darkness in life with expectation and awe.

Heartening, enchanting, and unflinchingly honest, *Starry-Eyed* will show you how to find the unexpected grace in your life as a woman, wife, mother, daughter, sister, and friend. Consider this your heart-to-heart sit-down with a woman who's been there and can help you find fresh eyes to see how beauty and pain can mingle with purpose.

Available in stores and online!

About MOPS International

You and me and the mom at the park and the mom in India—we have been placed in this time and space to raise the world together. Our purpose is the same, even when our day-to-day experiences are different.

Being a mom is beautiful and hard, and we get that sometimes you just need a safe space to breathe. A place to get some encouragement that what you are doing matters. MOPS is a movement helping women around the world to become leaders in their communities, to feel more equipped as moms, and to develop lifelong friendships.

MOPS

Connect with a group meeting near you at
www.mops.org/groupsearch.

. . .